Improving Thinking in the Classroom

Creating an Engaging, Exciting and Challenging Learning Environment

RALPH PIROZZO

© 2024 Ralph Pirozzo

This work is copyright. Apart from any pages identified as reproducible and any fair dealings for the purposes of private study, research, criticism or review, or as permitted under the Copyright Act, no part should be reproduced, transmitted, stored, communicated or recorded by any process, without written permission. Any pages identified as reproducible are only authorised for use in the classroom or by any school or nonprofit organisation that has purchased the book. Enquiries should be made to the publisher.

Published in 2024 by Amba Press, Melbourne, Australia.
www.ambapress.com.au

First published in 2005 by Hawker Brownlow Education.
A second edition was published in 2007 by Hawker Brownlow Education.
This edition replaces all previous editions.

ISBN: 9781923215009 (pbk)
ISBN: 9781923215016 (ebk)

A catalogue record for this book is available from the National Library of Australia.

Contents

Introduction 5
    Engaging all learners 8

Building the foundation 9
    Building depth and rigour using Bloom's taxonomy 9
    Engaging students with multiple intelligences 25
    Developing a 48 and 56-grid matrix that integrates multiple intelligences and Bloom's taxonomy 40

Applying the knowledge 45
    Using tools for improving thinking 45
    The thinking tool kit 46

**Transferring the knowledge to the real-world:
48 and 56-grid matrix** 73
    Real assessment tasks 73
    Core and elective 75
    Preparing a 48 and 56-grid matrix 77
    Example 1: Saving the koala 78
    Example 2: Out in space 80
    Example 3: Plants 84
    Case study 88

In conclusion 92
    Teachers' reflections on the 48 and 56-grid matrix 93

Appendix 96

Multiple Intelligences Test (MIT) 98

References 105

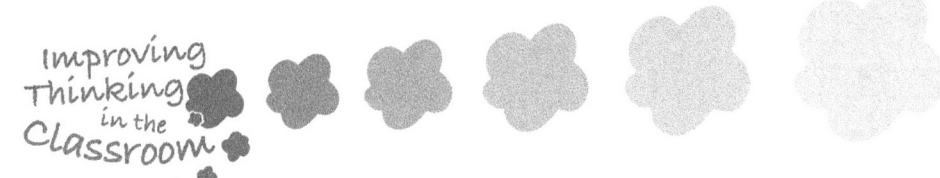

Introduction

Engagement, depth and rigour are essential characteristics of a curriculum that will motivate and interest students. This means challenging, meaningful and relevant activities that make the classroom an active centre of learning.

The rationale behind *Improving Thinking in the Classroom* is to provide teachers with useful and practical strategies that will enable them to create the most engaging, exciting and challenging learning environment for all their children.

Ralph's essentials of learning and teaching

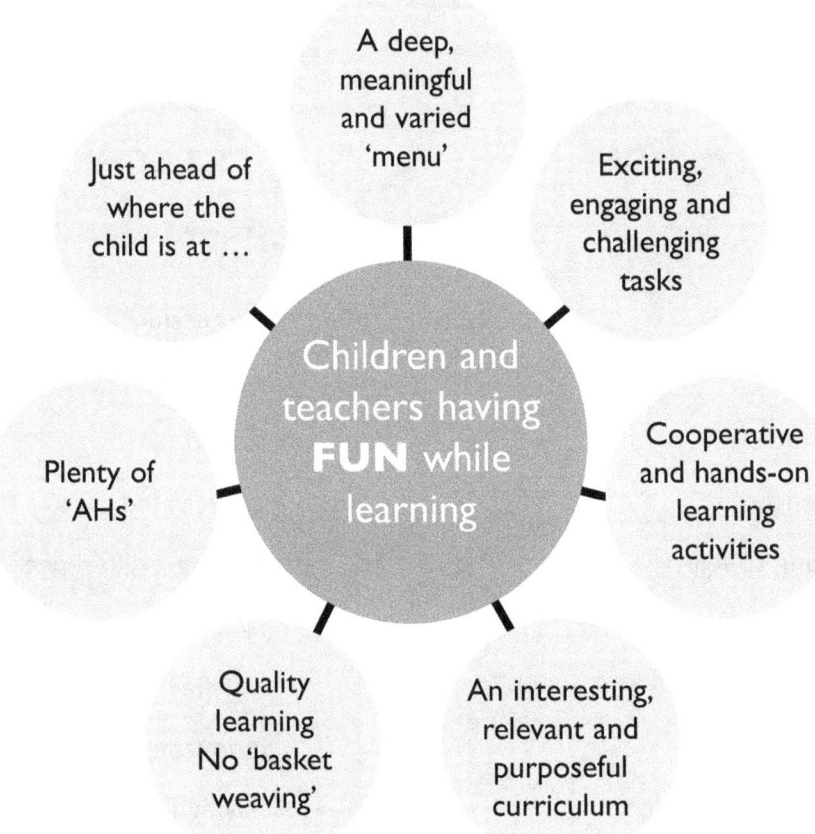

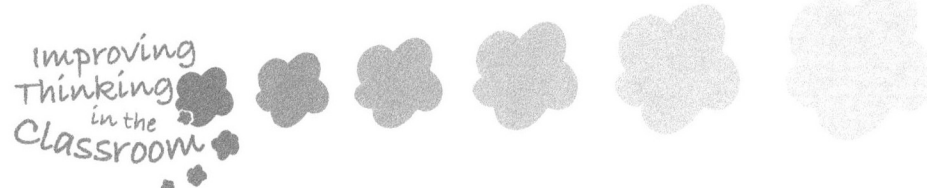

Ralph's essentials of learning and teaching will create a learning environment where students:

- are provided with learning activities/integrated projects that will nurture their thinking skills and cater for their individual characteristics of intelligence and learning
- become confident in applying various thinking tools to understand various concepts
- become engaged in learning and develop lifelong learning skills
- choose activities and tasks that they would like to do in order to complete a unit of work
- can focus on learning.

The benefits of implementing this thinking and engaging classroom will be confident, motivated students, wanting to rush back to the classroom the next day, and teachers will feel their teaching is valued and appreciated by their students.

The thinking and engaging classroom

CHILDREN

- happy
- confident
- motivated
- challenged
- wanting to learn
- high self-esteem
- enthusiastic
- self-directed
- having fun while learning

TEACHERS

- successful
- reflective
- valued
- appreciated
- making a difference
- facilitating
- satisfied
- innovating
- having fun while teaching

Introduction

In order to engage children, teachers need a framework. *Improving Thinking in the Classroom* is about developing a conceptual framework. This framework is unique because it enables us to align theory and practice in planning with the use of Bloom's taxonomy, multiple intelligences, thinking tools and cooperative learning strategies. This enables the development of integrated projects that feature:

- 48/56 activities based on the 48 and 56-grid matrix
- application of a variety of thinking tools
- cooperative learning activities and integrated projects culminating in real assessment tasks.

Ralph's conceptual framework of the thinking classroom

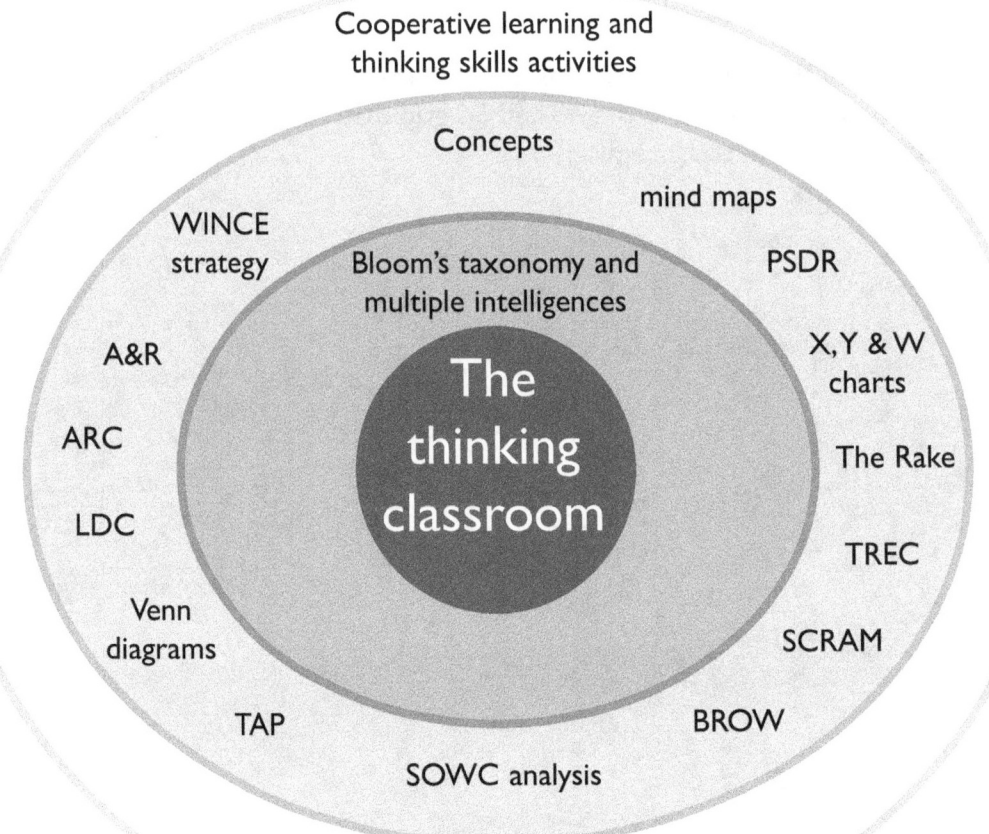

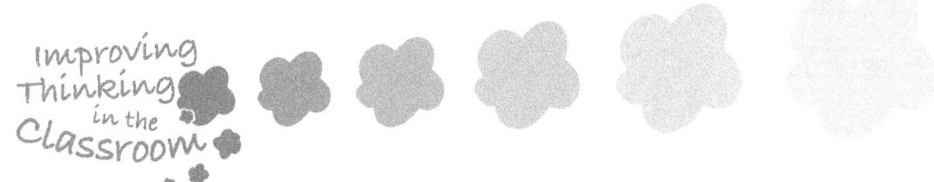

Engaging all learners

Planning and programming are essential factors in the successful classroom, but the vital question needs to be asked: what do we want to achieve through our planning and programming?

Undeniably, planning and programming must achieve two fundamental aims: it must nurture our students' thinking skills and simultaneously engage our children through their preferred learning styles.

Using this book will ensure that our lessons, units of work and activities will have these two major ingredients: 'engagement' and 'depth and rigour'.

The use of Bloom's cognitive taxonomy in the classroom provides depth and rigour. Using Bloom's 6 levels of thinking, teachers will be able to track the opportunities for students to engage in higher order thinking, thus enabling them to invigorate their units of work with more challenge.

The implementation of Gardner's 8 multiple intelligences, on the other hand, allows teachers to provide different ways of engaging students in thinking. Different ways of thinking are validated in the classroom as smart ways to work.

As is shown in the following sections, Bloom's taxonomy and Gardner's multiple intelligences, when combined in the 48 and 56-grid matrix, can change and recharge the atmosphere in your classroom!

Building the foundation

Building depth and rigour using Bloom's taxonomy

From the many available taxonomies, Bloom's taxonomy has been selected because it is very useful in planning students' learning outcomes at six different thinking levels ranging from Knowing to Evaluating.

In 1956, Benjamin Bloom led a group of educational psychologists in proposing that thinking behaviours can be measured along a continuum from simple to complex.

Bloom and his team identified the following three domains of educational activities: cognitive, affective and psychomotor. They pointed out that the cognitive domain deals with mental skills, the affective with feelings and emotions, while the psychomotor relates to manual or physical skills.

As we are particularly interested in nurturing thinking skills, we are going to concentrate only on the cognitive domain. This domain has been subdivided into six categories starting from the simplest behaviour to the most complex. The categories can be seen as degrees of difficulties. That is, the first one must be mastered before the next one can take place.

Considerable revision of Bloom's taxonomy was undertaken by a team lead by David Krathwohl (one of the authors of the original taxonomy) and Lorin Anderson in 1999. Changes included a deliberate attempt to ensure the taxonomy was useful in educational settings. Another significant change was that Knowledge was made separate because knowledge underpins all levels of thinking. Also, verbs were used to describe the cognitive domain. Evaluating was placed before Creating, although both are high-level thinking skills.

The table at the top of the following page reflects the change in the use of verbs to describe each of the levels of the taxonomy.

Original Bloom's taxonomy (1956)	Revised Bloom's taxonomy (1999)
EVALUATION	CREATING
SYNTHESIS	EVALUATING
ANALYSIS	ANALYSING
APPLICATION	APPLYING
COMPREHENSION	UNDERSTANDING
KNOWLEDGE	REMEMBERING ('Knowing' R. Pirozzo)

Improving Thinking in the Classroom will use a combination of the original and the revised Bloom's taxonomy. To summarise the two changes that have been made and provide reasons for the change:

1. Thinking is an active process. Unfortunately, words like Knowledge do not describe such an action and that is why we now use Knowing instead.

2. Young children and students with learning difficulties find it very difficult to deal with complex words like Comprehension and, in particular, Synthesis. Accordingly, these have been changed to Understanding and Creating respectively.

Other authors have argued that Evaluating should precede Creating. Yet, it is hard to imagine how a child could ever evaluate something that they have not created first. Therefore, in this author's view Creating should always precede Evaluating. This results in a slight readjustment of the revised taxonomy in favour of the old one:

Bloom's taxonomy
(adapted by R. Pirozzo, 2004)
Thinking strategies for all children

- Evaluating
- Creating
- Analysing
- Applying
- Understanding
- Knowing
- Pre-Knowing (R. Pirozzo)

Building the foundation

In summary, Bloom's taxonomy is extremely useful in providing a well-defined thinking framework. At the lower order levels (Knowing, Understanding and Applying) children are required to provide clearly defined answers to show how they can solve a problem based on what they already know and understand.

On the other hand, at the higher levels (Analysing, Creating and Evaluating) children are encouraged to apply critical thinking processes, thus developing higher order thinking skills (HOTS).

For example, at the Analysing level, children should be able to break knowledge into its various parts. At the Creating level we are more interested in the students re-assembling these parts and actually creating something new. Whereas, at the Evaluating level, we want our students to be able to discuss, evaluate and justify their opinions, decisions and recommendations.

This author has identified a need for the addition of an exciting sub-level to the Taxonomy, that is, the Pre-Knowing level (Pirozzo, 2004). This author believes this will cater specifically for the needs of children with learning difficulties, ESL students and children who come from families where the language is not 'elaborate'.

Why add Pre-Knowing to Bloom's Taxonomy?

The underlying philosophy of the original Bloom's Taxonomy (1956) was that all children commence their learning at the Knowing Level. This might have been the case in 1956, however it no longer reflects what teachers actually see in their classrooms today.

Undeniably, at present teachers are having to adjust significantly their programs and their effective learning & teaching strategies in order to cater for the needs of many children who do not arrive at school operating at the Knowing Level.

Included in this group are children with learning difficulties, ESL students and K-1 children who come from families where the language is not "elaborate".

Given the fact that these children are presently not operating at the Knowing Level, often they are referred to specialist teachers for remediation and intervention programs.

Undoubtedly, these remediation and intervention programs aim at enriching the learning environment of these children to enable them to deal successfully with the material presented at the Knowing Level.

In doing so, teachers are constantly "digging" deeper into their own experiences in order to "bridge" these children's learning with the expectations of the classroom. In doing so, teachers are scaffolding these children at a new level, the Pre-Knowing Level.

The concept of the Pre-Knowing Level was first proposed by Ralph Pirozzo in 2004.

Thus, the Pre-Knowing Level needs to be added to the original Bloom's Taxonomy. This should not be seen in any way as to undermine the value of Bloom's Taxonomy. Basically, this change reflects the reality of today's classroom.

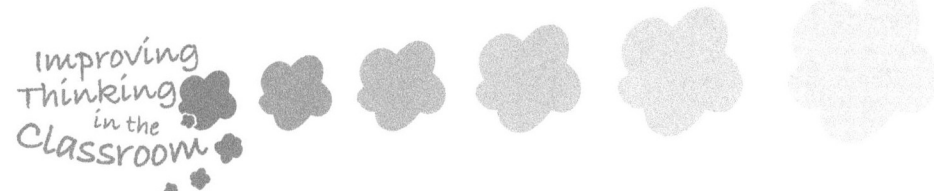

Ralph's BAT learning model

The BAT model

It is important to operate an 'open door policy' in relation to students moving within the various levels (note the arrows in the Teaching Wheel on p. 13). Children begin their journey at different levels rather than always commencing at the lowest level. Students do not need to remain glued in one particular level forever, but rather, they can be engaged by introducing a problem that requires them to seek knowledge.

Keep in mind the students who, when asked to build their own bridges using plastic straws, quickly jump to the building stage without worrying too much about investigating the best structural design. Eventually, their bridges collapse to the ground because they have not bothered to strengthen their pillars. Then, they finally decide to discuss this within the group and find out that triangular shapes will give them the most strength. What these students have learned is that the tallest skyscraper will

Building the foundation

The Teaching Wheel
(devised by R. Pirozzo, 2004, based on Bloom's Taxonomy)

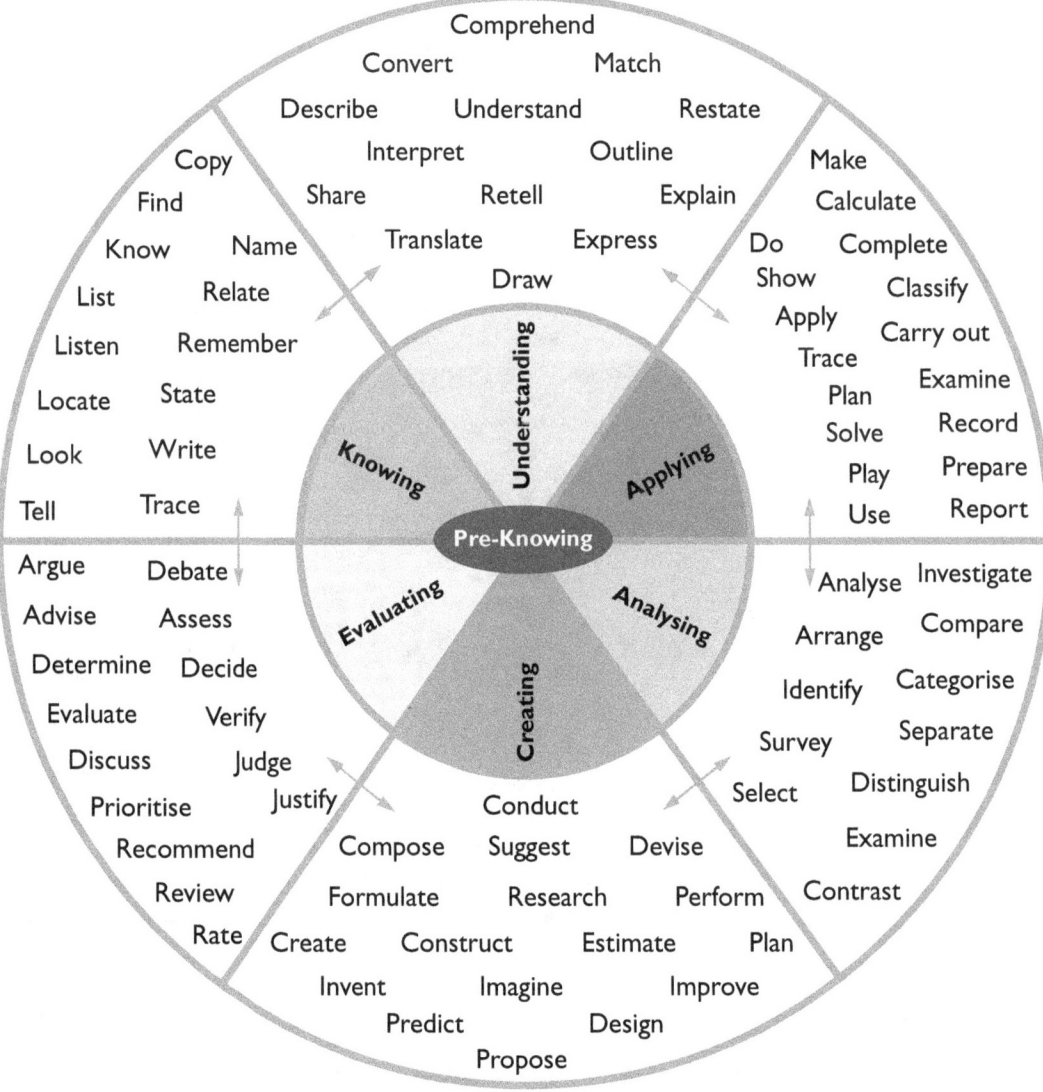

collapse if it has a poor foundation. Indeed, the students learn to value the lower order thinking as an important part of their learning, and so this opportunity for inquiry becomes a crucial part of a well-thoughtout thinking skills program.

This is summarised in the learning model (below and p. 12) because it promotes learning at three different levels:

> Level 1: Building the foundation (Knowing and Understanding).
>
> Level 2: Applying the knowledge (Applying and Analysing).
>
> Level 3: Transferring the knowledge to solve 'real-world' issues (Creating and Evaluating).

The Learning & Teaching Wheel

(devised by R. Pirozzo, 2005, based on Bloom's Taxonomy)

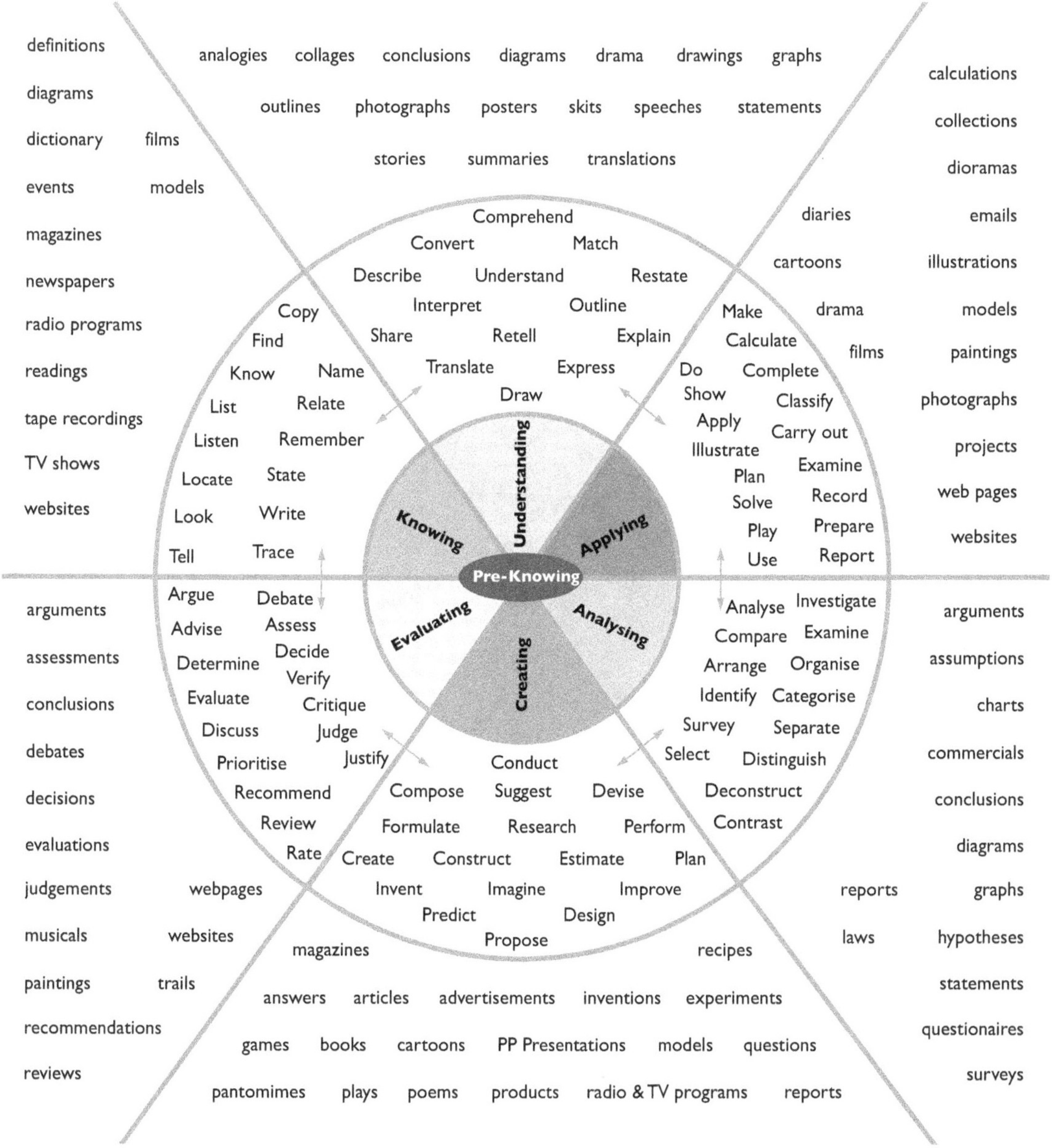

definitions
diagrams
dictionary   films
events   models
magazines
newspapers
radio programs
readings
tape recordings
TV shows
websites

analogies collages conclusions diagrams drama drawings graphs
outlines photographs posters skits speeches statements
stories summaries translations

Comprehend
Convert   Match
Describe Understand Restate
Interpret   Outline
Copy   Share   Retell   Explain
Find   Translate   Express
Know Name   Draw
List Relate
Listen Remember
Locate State
Look Write
Tell Trace

Knowing | Understanding | Applying
Pre-Knowing
Evaluating | Creating | Analysing

Argue Debate
Advise Assess
Decide
Determine Verify
Evaluate Critique
Discuss Judge
Prioritise Justify
Recommend Compose Suggest Devise
Review Formulate Research Perform
Rate Create Construct Estimate Plan
Invent Imagine Improve
Predict Design
Propose

diaries
cartoons

Make   drama
Calculate   films
Do Complete
Show   Classify
Apply Carry out
Illustrate Examine
Plan
Solve Record
Play Prepare
Use Report

Analyse Investigate
Compare Examine
Arrange Organise
Identify Categorise
Survey Separate
Select Distinguish
Deconstruct
Contrast

calculations
collections
dioramas
emails
illustrations
models
paintings
photographs
projects
web pages
websites

arguments
assumptions
charts
commercials
conclusions
diagrams

arguments
assessments
conclusions
debates
decisions
evaluations
judgements
musicals
paintings
recommendations
reviews

webpages
websites
trails

magazines
answers articles advertisements inventions experiments
games books cartoons PP Presentations models questions
pantomimes plays poems products radio & TV programs reports

reports
laws
recipes

graphs
hypotheses
statements
questionaires
surveys

Introducing Bloom's into the classroom

What the original Bloom's taxonomy did not provide us with, however, are the verbs, sample questions and learning activities that we can use to nurture our children's thinking skills from low level to high level. For that we need to go to The Learning and Teaching Wheel (p. 14) and Bloom's Taxonomy sample questions (pp. 15–20). Please note that The Learning and Teaching Wheel has been devised specifically to enable children to select the activities that they would like to complete.

Building the foundation

The Learning and Teaching Wheel illustrates that throughout the school day we need to take our children on a journey from low-level to high-level thinking and that these verbs will help us in asking questions that will encourage critical thinking.

Now that we have the verbs relating to Bloom's six thinking levels, we can return to our planning and programming and use them to generate a large number of questions and activities as shown in the following tables.

Bloom's taxonomy: Knowing
Sample questions and learning activities

Thinking level	Knowing
Useful verbs	Copy Listen Relate Trace Find Locate Remember Write Know Look State List Name Tell
Sample questions	• Can you name the …? • Look at this and then … • Find the meaning of … • How many times …? • What happened after …? • What is the name of …? • Who was the boy that …? • Which is the right answer? • Where do you live?
Learning activities	• List all the people in the story. • Locate all the information that you can about World War II. • Listen to your teacher. • Look at the clock and tell the time. • Find the meaning of this word in the dictionary. • Write the formula for photosynthesis. • Name the capital of Indonesia. • Copy the homework from the board. • Trace this picture from the textbook. • Remember what we learned yesterday! • Tell your group what we need for this activity. • State clearly what the character said in the story.

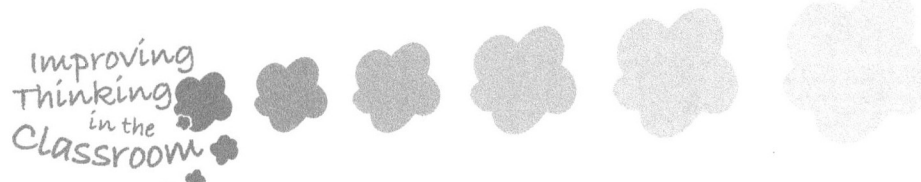

Bloom's taxonomy: Understanding
Sample questions and learning activities

Thinking level	Understanding			
Useful verbs	Comprehend	Explain	Outline	Translate
	Convert	Express	Restate	Understand
	Draw	Interpret	Retell	
	Describe	Match	Share	
Sample questions	• Can you write the formula for … in your own words …? • Can you convert this to that? • Can you give an example of …? • Can you write a brief outline of …? • Can you match these two lists?		• What do you think could have happened next in the story? • What was the main idea …? • Who do you think stole the …? • Who was the main character? • How do you say this word in French?	
Learning activities	• Convert this word problem into a mathematical statement. • Draw pictures to show how plants and animals interact together. • Outline your plans for your next project. • Explain the meaning of this symbol. • Express how you feel in your own words. • Draw a diagram/map/plan. • Match these two lists. • Restate the story in your own words. • Describe what the author meant. • Retell this from the point of view of the villain. • Share your drawings with your group. • Translate this sentence from English into French.			

Building the foundation

Bloom's taxonomy: Applying
Sample questions and learning activities

Thinking level	Applying				
Useful verbs	Apply	Complete	Make	Record	Use
	Calculate	Do	Plan	Report	
	Classify	Examine	Play	Show	
	Carry out	Illustrate	Prepare	Solve	
Sample questions	• Can you calculate the number of tiles needed to cover this? • Can you classify the following animals into their proper Phyla? • Can you construct a rectangle with the following dimensions …?		• Can you plan and conduct an experiment? • From the information provided, can you develop a set of instructions on how to operate …? • Can you construct a model of …?		
Learning activities	• Show in a chart where all the plants are found in your suburb. • Complete the following sentence … • Construct a food chain using these animals. • Classify the following organisms into their correct Phyla. • Illustrate the main ideas of the book. • Make a clay model of a volcano. • Calculate how many metres of wire is needed to fence the following paddock. • Solve the following maths problems and show all your calculations. • Examine this statement from the bully's point of view. • Complete this flow chart showing the various stages of bread making. • Carry out this chemical experiment.				

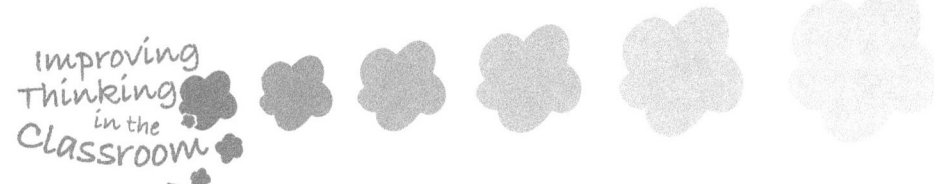

Bloom's taxonomy: Analysing
Sample questions and learning activities

Thinking level	Analysing		
Useful verbs	Analyse Arrange Categorise Compare	Contrast Distinguish Examine Identify	Investigate Select Separate Survey
Sample questions	<ul><li>Which events could not have happened? Why?</li><li>How is this similar/different …?</li><li>How would the story have ended if …?</li><li>Can you distinguish between …?</li><li>What was the turning point in the play?</li><li>Can you explain what must have happened when …?</li><li>Are there other possible outcomes?</li><li>Are there other motives behind …?</li><li>Can you identify the robber?</li></ul>		
Learning activities	<ul><li>Compare and contrast Asian and African elephants.</li><li>Identify the strengths of this commercial.</li><li>Categorise these items into plastic and metal.</li><li>Construct a graph to illustrate the following relationship …</li><li>Survey your friends in terms of their eating habits.</li><li>Arrange these numbers from the largest to the smallest.</li><li>Investigate how this discovery can be used.</li><li>Analyse a work of art in terms of form, colour and texture.</li><li>Select the best music for this play.</li><li>Investigate how we can reduce bullying.</li><li>Separate oil from water.</li></ul>		

Building the foundation

Bloom's taxonomy: Creating
Sample questions and learning activities

Thinking level	Creating			
Useful verbs	Compose	Design	Imagine	Predict
	Conduct	Devise	Improve	Propose
	Construct	Estimate	Invent	Suggest
	Create	Formulate	Perform	Research
Sample questions	• Can you create new uses for …? • If you had access to all the necessary resources, how would you deal with …? • Can you invent a possible solution to …? • Can you develop a proposal which would …? • How many ways can you devise to …? • Can you propose how we could improve this experiment? • Can you predict what will happen if …?			
Learning activities	• Create a new product and plan a marketing campaign for it. • Propose how you will improve this … • Invent a machine to accomplish a special task. • Design a cover for a magazine. • Compose a rhythm or add new words to a well-known tune. • Construct a model of the DNA molecule. • Predict what will happen when … • Suggest ways to improve the following … • Conduct a survey to gather information about teenage smoking. • Research how we can reduce world poverty. • Estimate the cost of this marketing campaign.			

Bloom's taxonomy: Evaluating
Sample questions and learning activities

Thinking level	Evaluating			
Useful verbs	Advise	Decide	Judge	Recommend
	Argue	Determine	Justify	Review
	Assess	Discuss	Prioritise	Verify
	Debate	Evaluate	Rate	
Sample questions	• How would you defend your position in relation to …? • What do you think about …? • Can you assess and choose a better solution to …? • How would you have handled …?		• What changes would you recommend? Why? • Do you believe that …? • How would you feel if …? • How ineffective are …? • What is the most valuable …?	
Learning activities	• Justify why you have chosen this particular piece of music for your school play. • Discuss factors that should be considered when buying toys for young children. • Verify that this is in fact the right answer. • Debate: Should Australia mine uranium? • Determine if this novel is suitable for high school students. • Verify that this maths formula is correct. • Evaluate the research on AIDS. • Judge which is the best short story. • Decide on the criteria to judge a speech. • Review this book and rate it from 1 to 10. • Recommend new strategies to be adopted based on your SOWC analysis.			

Adapted by Ralph Pirozzo (2001) with permission of the Department of Education, Employment and Training, Victoria.

These sample questions and learning activities are able to be integrated into existing thinking skills program, thus, continuing to further nurture children's thinking from low level to high level.

Building the foundation

Preparing a unit plan

This material now becomes the basis for preparing a unit plan. At first glance this appears to be a standard unit plan. In fact, most unit plans commence by identifying the students' learning outcomes, followed by the assessment items and finishing with the learning experiences. But how do you know that these learning experiences are going to nurture all your children's thinking skills? How do you know that these learning experiences have some depth and rigour? Often, these questions are answered by relying on what can best be described as 'gut' feelings.

Rather than relying on 'gut' feelings, Bloom's taxonomy can be used to build depth and rigour in your lesson plans. On this unit plan the verbs from Bloom's taxonomy have been added to the last column in an abbreviated mode: K (Knowing), U (Understanding), Ap (Applying), An (Analysing), C (Creating) and E (Evaluating).

Unit plan							
Year level:		Key learning area:						
Topic:							
Students' learning outcomes	Assessment	Learning experiences	K	U	Ap	An	C	E

So far, you have not been invited to actually work with this material. It is crucial that you get the opportunity to practise using it. Thus, in order to complete Bloom's taxonomy: Activity 1, read the students' learning experiences, then look at The Teaching Wheel (p. 13). Find where the relevant verb is located and then place a tick under the appropriate thinking level e.g. K, U, Ap, An, C or E.

For example, in completing the student learning activity titled, 'List all the people in the story', we will find that 'List' is located under Knowing. Therefore, we will place a tick under K (Knowing).

Once you have completed these activities, turn to pp. 96–97 to check your work.

Bloom's taxonomy: Activity 1

Students' learning experiences	K	U	Ap	An	C	E
1. List all the people in the story.						
2. Evaluate the research on AIDS.						
3. Name the capital of Indonesia.						
4. Locate all the parks in your suburb.						
5. Look at the clock and tell me the time.						
6. Retell this from the point view of the villain.						
7. Draw pictures to show how plants and animals interact together.						
8. Illustrate the main ideas of the book.						
9. Complete a flow chart showing the various stages of bread making.						
10. Design a cover for a magazine.						
11. Convert this word problem into a mathematical statement.						
12. Outline your plans for your next project.						
13. Construct an ecological foodchain and foodweb.						
14. Classify the following organisms into their correct Phyla.						
15. Make a clay model of a volcano.						
16. Survey your friends in terms of their eating habits.						
17. Solve the following maths problem and show all your calculations.						
18. Make a scrapbook about …						
19. Translate this sentence from English into French.						
20. Write your home address.						
21. Recommend new strategies to be adopted based on your SOWC analysis.						
22. Categorise these items into plastic and metal.						

Building the foundation

Students learning experiences (cont.)	K	U	Ap	An	C	E
23. Make a family tree showing all the important relationships.						
24. Compare and contrast Asian and African elephants.						
25. Determine whether this novel is suitable for secondary school students.						
26. Review a work of art in terms of form, colour and texture.						
27. Construct a graph to illustrate the following relationship.						
28. Devise a number of ways to improve …						
29. Calculate how many metres of wire is needed to fence a paddock with the following dimensions …						
30. Invent a machine that will be able to do a certain task.						
31. Compose a rhythm or add new words to a well-known tune.						
32. Devise an experiment that will extract more iron from its ore.						
33. Write the formula for photosynthesis.						
34. Retell the story in your own words.						
35. Design a solar energy car.						
36. Conduct a survey to gather information about teenage smoking.						
37. Organise and conduct a debate dealing with a controversial issue.						
38. Discuss factors that should be considered when buying toys for your children.						
39. Justify why you have chosen this particular piece of music for your school play						
40. List all the information that you remember about the Second World War.						
41. Make a flowchart to show the critical stages of …						
42. Construct a model of the DNA molecule.						

Whether your answers are exactly the same as those on pages 96–97 is not the real issue. The real issue is that without using Bloom's taxonomy as quality control you could easily develop activities that do not challenge your students with appropriate depth and rigour.

Bloom's taxonomy of cognitive skills provides a sound basis for evaluating and planning the level of thinking in the classroom. Using a range of activities in our unit plans, which combine both higher and lower order thinking, will provide an environment for the development of thinking skills and challenge all learners with activities that are appropriate to their learning needs.

Reflection on Bloom's taxonomy

Whilst Bloom's taxonomy is great in nurturing children's thinking skills, it does not provide for the different learning styles of all students. Basically, this means that if Bloom's taxonomy is used alone there is a very good chance that there will be many children who will not engage with the activities and lessons that have been prepared for them. Inevitably, many of these disengaged students will cause you to spend an enormous amount of time dealing with discipline problems rather than doing what you do best – teaching.

So, how can we engage children in their learning?

Building the foundation

Engaging students with multiple intelligences

A very powerful theory that should enable teachers to engage children through their preferred learning styles is multiple intelligences (MI). Multiple intelligences is a widely accepted theory on which to base classroom practice.

In 1983, Howard Gardner proposed a new view of intelligence that has been defined as 'the capacity to solve problems or to fashion products that are valued in one or more cultural setting' (Gardner & Hatch 1989).

Using both biological and cultural research, Gardner (1983) postulated that there are at least seven intelligences. Then, in 1999 he added an eighth intelligence, the Naturalist:

 • **Verbal–linguistic intelligence**

 • **Logical–mathematical intelligence**

 • **Visual–spatial intelligence**

 • **Body–kinesthetic intelligence**

 • **Musical–rhythmic intelligence**

 • **Interpersonal–social intelligence**

 • **Intrapersonal–intuitive intelligence**

 • **Naturalist intelligence**

In addition, Gardner (1999) has indicated the possibility of other intelligences such as a ninth intelligence, the existential.

One of the key features of the theory of multiple intelligences is the recognition that people can be smart in different ways.

Pages 26–33 lists each intelligence along with a brief description of how individuals who possess these intelligences learn best.

Verbal–linguistic intelligence

Children with a well-developed verbal–linguistic intelligence learn best by reading, writing and speaking. These children use words to:

- communicate with other people through written and spoken words
- entertain others by telling stories and jokes
- express feelings and emotions
- make speeches and argue their point of views
- learn a new language.

Given the fact that these children learn best by 'using words', what activities strengthen their verbal–linguistic intelligence?

- reading and writing stories, jokes, poems and plays
- holding discussions and debates
- enhancing public speaking and interviewing skills
- completing and creating puzzles, word and spelling games
- writing and editing a class magazine
- keeping a personal journal and/or diary
- creating a newspaper, magazine, radio, Internet and TV advertisement
- using various thinking tools such as brainstorming, LDC, TAP and BROW
- giving children opportunities to create their own stories, poetry, plays and debates as an integral part of the unit, and then encouraging them to share their creations with their class
- attending plays and drama productions whenever possible

Building the foundation

Logical–mathematical intelligence

Children with a well-developed logical–mathematical intelligence learn best by working with numbers and science. These children use numbers and reasoning skills to:

- solve mathematical problems
- recognise and categorise abstract patterns and relationships in a sequential way
- classify plants and animals
- think logically in order to figure out why things work the way they do.

Given the fact that these children learn best by 'reasoning', what activities strengthen their logical–mathematical intelligence?

- carrying out many different types of mathematical calculations
- analysing and interpreting data
- using computers to make calculations and spreadsheets
- creating computer programs
- performing many science experiments
- collecting plant and animal specimens and classifying them
- giving children opportunities to create their own computer programs and science experiments as an integral part of the unit
- using various thinking tools such as concept maps, the PSDR method, WINCE, SCRAM and TREC

Visual–spatial intelligence

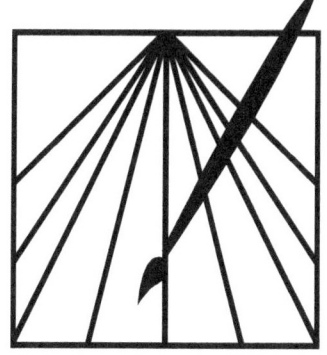

Children with a well-developed visual–spatial intelligence learn best by painting, drawing and visualising. These children use images and pictures to:

- communicate with other people through visual means such as paintings, drawings, sketches, maps, graphs and charts
- create accurate maps and graphic designs
- create vivid mental images of where words and pictures are placed on a page
- show their emotions by making excellent use of facial expressions.

Given the fact that these children learn best by 'seeing images and pictures', what activities strengthen their visual–spatial intelligence?

- painting, drawing and sketching
- drawing diagrams and graphs
- preparing flyers, posters, collages, maps, mazes and murals
- having access to art books, photos, puzzles, videos and films
- illustrating books, reports, magazines, newsletters
- designing the graphics for a newspaper, magazine, radio, Internet and TV advertisement
- giving children opportunities to create their own paintings, drawings, flyers, posters, collages, maps, mazes, murals, videos and films as an integral part of their unit
- using various thinking tools such as Venn diagrams, The Rake and X, Y & W charts
- visiting art galleries and museums whenever possible

Building the foundation

Body–kinesthetic intelligence

Children with a well developed body–kinesthetic intelligence learn best by doing hands-on activities, sports and dance. These children use body movements to:

- communicate by creating new forms of expressions such as dancing
- perform physical activities showing coordination, speed and flexibility
- communicate feelings through body language and imitating others
- use tools to build and repair various items
- constantly experiment with objects to see how things work.

Given the fact that these children learn best by 'doing', what activities strengthen their body–kinesthetic Intelligence?

- regularly giving these children the opportunity to learn by using their hands to build models, games, crafts and props
- practising and playing sports and physical exercises
- learning dances from various cultural groups
- maintaining gardens and rainforest areas
- performing role plays and act out scenes
- carrying out various science experiments
- participating in swimming, athletics and sports carnivals
- giving children opportunities to create their own dance as an integral part of their unit, and then, encouraging them to perform their dance in front of their class
- taking children on excursions and attending sporting events, dance competitions and crafts shows whenever possible

Musical–rhythmic intelligence

Children with a well-developed musical–rhythmic intelligence learn best by listening and making music. These children use music and rhythm to:

- communicate with others by expressing and responding through music
- remember tunes and melodies
- play a musical instrument
- sing and create new songs, jingles, operas, performances and compositions.

Given the fact that these children learn best by 'hearing musical sounds', what activities strengthen their musical–rhythmic intelligence?

- playing baroque music whilst the children are working cooperatively on projects
- listening to music that is related to the unit being studied
- teaching through songs, sounds effects and jingles
- having a variety of musical instruments, tapes, CDs, soundtracks and tapes available in the classroom
- accessing specialist music teachers so that the children can learn how to play a musical instrument
- composing music on computers
- establishing choirs, music clubs and music bands
- giving children opportunities to create their own songs, melodies, sound effects, raps and jingles as an integral part of their unit, and then, encouraging them to perform their creations in front of their class
- attending various concerts whenever possible.

Building the foundation

Interpersonal–social intelligence

Children with a well-developed interpersonal–social intelligence learn best by working with others. These children use this ability to:

- interact, cooperate, organise and lead other people
- empathise with others
- inspire others to achieve a common goal
- resolve conflicts and build relationships.

Given the fact that these children learn best by 'working with others', what activities strengthen their interpersonal–social intelligence?

- completing projects by working cooperatively
- employing various thinking tools such as TPS, TPSS, Jigsaw and the SOWC analysis
- providing and receiving feedback using the LDC thinking tool
- doing drama and role-plays
- coaching younger children in all areas of the curriculum including reading, writing and mathematics
- volunteering to work with community groups such as the local senior citizen's home
- establishing social clubs and committees
- discussing and debating controversial issues
- developing interview and conflict resolutions skills
- making learning fun by allowing the children to play games and to celebrate important events like birthdays

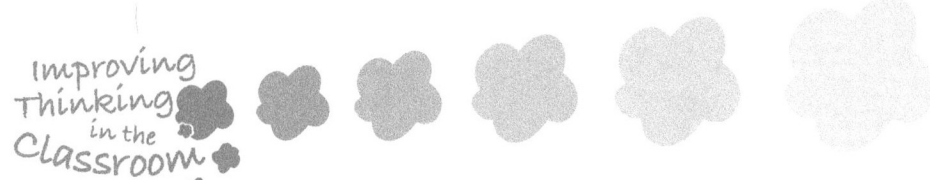

Intrapersonal–intuitive Intelligence

Children with a well-developed intrapersonal–intuitive intelligence learn best by working alone. These children use this ability to:

- assess their emotions, strengths and weaknesses
- express strong emotions and well-developed opinions
- set goals in a single-minded manner
- form conceptual frameworks to explain what is going on

Given the fact that these children learn best by 'working alone', what activities strengthen their intrapersonal–intuitive intelligence?

- completing projects independently by using a variety of delivery systems such as self-study, self-paced projects, structured units and individualised programs
- using learning contracts so that children will have the opportunity to choose the activities that they would like to do
- employing various thinking tools such as concept maps, mind maps, A&R, ARC, LDC, TAP, SOWC analysis and 'My area of control'
- preparing journals, diaries and autobiographies
- setting up learning centres so that children can choose various areas to work in
- providing time for meditation, setting up goals and personal reflection

Naturalist intelligence

Children with a well-developed naturalist intelligence learn best by relying on their strong connections to nature. These children use this ability to:

- care for plants and animals
- recognise parts of the natural world such as rock and cloud formations
- speak out for the rights and preservation of plants and animals
- conserve natural resources to achieve sustainable growth
- become involved in planting projects, recycling centres and global environmental issues.

Given the fact that these children learn best by 'making connection with nature', what activities strengthen their naturalistic intelligence?

- having a pet in the classroom so that the children can observe and note its behaviour, food intake and growth
- encouraging the children to tend plants either in the classroom or by establishing a small garden
- organising excursions, nature walks and visits to museums
- collecting and classifying natural specimens (insects, leaves, flowers and rocks) by using magnifiers, microscopes, telescopes and binoculars, and then setting up various collections
- establishing a weather station so that children can study how to forecast the temperature and rainfall.
- establishing an environmental club and a recycling program
- encouraging discussions, debates and presentations relating to conservation issues
- reading stories and watching shows that deal with animals and natural events
- keeping reference books relating to biology, astronomy, meteorology and zoology in the classroom
- organising individual nature portfolio to store their animal and plant specimens, field notes, photos and drawings

Some of the characteristics of the theory of multiple intelligences

By relying on brain research and medical case studies, Gardner asserted that:

- each of these intelligences is located in one or more particular areas of the brain
- all human beings possess all eight intelligences in various amounts
- each person has a different intellectual composition. In other words, we do not have the same strength in each intelligence.

Although the intelligences are located in different parts of the brain, Gardner claims that the eight intelligences rarely operate independently. Rather they are used simultaneously and complement each other as we learn to develop skills and solve problems. For example, a ballerina needs to interpret the music (musical–rhythmic intelligence), work cooperatively with other dancers (interpersonal intelligence), inspire her audience with her passion for dancing (intrapersonal intelligence) and complete the required movements with style (bodily–kinesthetic intelligence).

Undeniably, the theory of multiple intelligences further supports the notion that each individual is unique. Thus, in the same way that we look different from one another, have different kinds of personalities, and have our own talents, gifts and abilities, we also think differently. In other words, we have different kinds of brains.

Are multiple intelligences and learning styles related?

If children have different cognitive strengths, does this mean that they also have different cognitive styles? Do they learn in different ways to other people?

Once it is recognised that each student has their own unique set of intellectual strengths and weaknesses, teachers are then in a position to structure the way we present new material to engage all our children's intelligences.

In order to do this we need to determine how a child learns new material when it is presented through various effective learning and teaching strategies. How a child processes this new material, is referred to as the child's learning style!

Armstrong (1994) summarised this by saying 'a person's learning style is the intelligence at work.'

A powerful analogy can be gathered from biological sciences. Every species' characteristics are dictated by genes. Basically, genes, are responsible for 'who we are' and they control our every characteristic, including such things as height, weight and hair colour. Even though we are unable to see the genes we can certainly see the expression of the genes – in the way we look, how tall or short we are and the way we behave.

Similarly, we cannot see a child's intelligences because they are located in the brain. The theory of multiple intelligences is a cognitive theory but it does not directly provide us with the children's learning styles. However, we can certainly observe how a child reacts when presented with different types of information. Therefore, we can argue that a child's learning styles are determined by their developed multiple intelligences or their intelligence profile.

If different children learn best by talking and reasoning, or looking and doing, or cooperating and reflecting, or caring for the environment, then we can use this information to teach these children.

For example, should a child have a highly developed visual–spatial intelligence, this will tell us that this child represents things spatially, tends to think in pictures and needs to create mental images to retain information. In terms of learning styles, we can confidently say that this child is a visual learner. This information now enables us to select many pathways to provide for this student's developed visual–spatial intelligence. This rich and varied menu will include drawings, paintings, maps, graphs, photos, charts, mazes, puzzles, videos, films and the use of various thinking tools such as X, Y & W charts and Venn diagrams.

Then, we can use these strengths to help students become more successful in other areas of study. For example, we may help a child who has a highly developed bodily–kinesthetic intelligence to learn English? On the other hand, another student who has a highly developed linguistic intelligence may be able to use another path to learn how to solve mathematics problems.

Indeed, one of the most remarkable features of the theory of multiple intelligences is how it provides us with at least eight different potential pathways to engage children. Thus, if a child is having difficulty learning some material through the linguistic or logical way of instruction, we then have at least another six ways that we can present this material in order to facilitate learning.

For example, in teaching the solar system through a teacher-directed mode, we often find that very soon many children switch off whilst we are dealing with the names and sizes of the planets and their respective distance from the sun. Often these disengaged children commence talking and to do everything possible to annoy both the teacher and the other students.

However, these same disengaged students come alive and become engaged in learning the moment we ask them to draw and to build a space station! Interestingly, in building their space station these students will rely on the same data that they refused to learn from a lecture. The major difference is that now this information is relevant because it will enable them to decide where and how to build their space station.

There is no denying that in many classrooms, disengaged children often become discipline problems. The good news is that by providing for the children's developed multiple intelligences, engagement will increase whilst discipline problems will decrease.

Introducing multiple intelligences in the classroom

By teaching for multiple intelligences in the classrooms, we are sending a very clear message to the children – that is, that we value at least eight ways to be smart.

This will increase the enjoyment of learning for all children including those who may not be very successful in the more traditional subjects like reading and mathematics. Yet, these children may have a real gift for music, sports, dance, painting, drawing and building through cooperative learning, hands-on activities and caring for the environment. Similarly, our bright children will have the opportunity to spend much more time in deepening and broadening their knowledge in the areas of interest to them.

Some of the best ways to commence using this material is to map your own preferred multiple intelligences by placing a number from 1 (the area that you enjoy working in the most) to 8 (the area that you enjoy working in the least) on The Engaging Wheel (p. 37). After this you can gauge (roughly) your children's preferred multiple intelligences by asking them to complete this chart in the same way that you have done.

Please note that a new multiple intelligence test has been devised by Ralph Pirozzo (2006). You will find a copy of this test on p. 98.

Once we have this general overview we are in a position to start asking a rather relevant question: are we presently engaging all the children through their preferred learning styles?

Obviously, if a teacher has strengths in four of the eight multiple intelligences they will still need to ignite the learning potential of those students who show interest and have strengths in other areas.

Applying the Engaging Wheel (p. 38) enables teachers to engage those children who have strengths in different areas than themselves by selecting various activities from this chart.

Building the foundation

The engaging wheel
(devised by R. Pirozzo, 2003, based on The Theory of Multiple Intelligences (Gardner, 1983, 1999))

- I enjoy caring for plants and animals.
- I enjoy reading, writing and speaking.
- I enjoy working with numbers and science.
- I enjoy working by myself.
- I enjoy working with others.
- I enjoy painting, drawing and visualising.
- I enjoy making and listening to music
- I enjoy doing hands-on activities, sports and dance.

Applying the engaging wheel

(devised by R. Pirozzo, 2003, based on The Theory of Multiple Intelligences (Gardner, 1983, 1999))

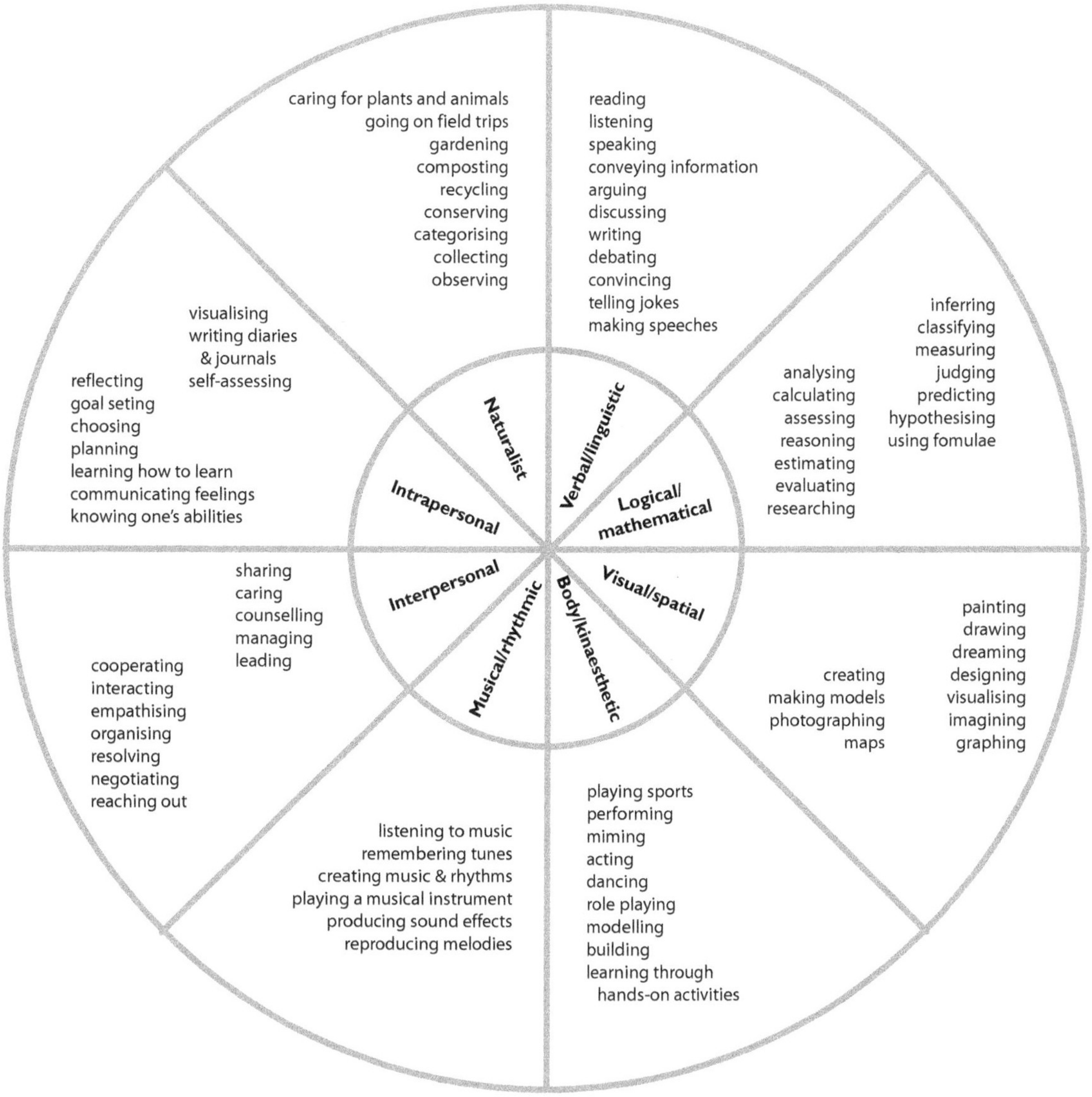

Naturalist
- caring for plants and animals
- going on field trips
- gardening
- composting
- recycling
- conserving
- categorising
- collecting
- observing

Verbal/linguistic
- reading
- listening
- speaking
- conveying information
- arguing
- discussing
- writing
- debating
- convincing
- telling jokes
- making speeches

Logical/mathematical
- analysing
- calculating
- assessing
- reasoning
- estimating
- evaluating
- researching
- inferring
- classifying
- measuring
- judging
- predicting
- hypothesising
- using formulae

Visual/spatial
- creating
- making models
- photographing
- maps
- painting
- drawing
- dreaming
- designing
- visualising
- imagining
- graphing

Body/kinaesthetic
- playing sports
- performing
- miming
- acting
- dancing
- role playing
- modelling
- building
- learning through hands-on activities

Musical/rhythmic
- listening to music
- remembering tunes
- creating music & rhythms
- playing a musical instrument
- producing sound effects
- reproducing melodies

Interpersonal
- sharing
- caring
- counselling
- managing
- leading
- cooperating
- interacting
- empathising
- organising
- resolving
- negotiating
- reaching out

Intrapersonal
- visualising
- writing diaries & journals
- self-assessing
- reflecting
- goal setting
- choosing
- planning
- learning how to learn
- communicating feelings
- knowing one's abilities

Building the foundation

Reflections on multiple intelligences

While multiple intelligences enables you to cater for students' unique learning styles it does not assist directly in building depth and rigour in units, lessons and activities.

For example, in some classrooms where multiple intelligences has been used as the only planning and teaching model, we find that a number of students, including some of our bright children, choose to complete low-level activities thus becoming engaged in surface learning. Unfortunately, this leads these children to produce huge amounts of fluffy material that has very little depth and rigour.

Bloom's taxonomy has the capacity to nurture children's thinking skills through six different thinking levels whilst the theory of multiple intelligences provides the opportunity to engage students through at least eight different ways of learning.

Thus, given the strengths and limitations of these two models, we can get the best of both worlds by integrating Bloom's taxonomy and multiple intelligences and thus having at least 48/56 activities with which to nurture and engage children.

  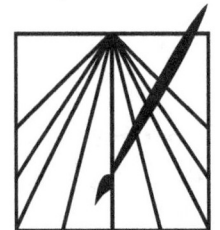 

Developing a 48 and 56-grid matrix that integrates multiple intelligences and Bloom's taxonomy

The primary value of the 48-grid matrix is deliberate in its design to nurture children's thinking skills from low level (Knowing) to high level (Evaluating) and simultaneously to engage students through their preferred learning styles.

Undeniably, the multiple intelligences and Bloom's taxonomy matrix provides us with a framework where we can embed our thinking tools (Section two) thus directing the children to use the most appropriate tools in order to solve a particular problem or issue.

On the following two pages you will find a blank 48 and 56-grid matrix that clearly labels the eight multiple intelligences running along the left hand column and the six thinking levels from Bloom's taxonomy along the top row. The fourth matrix on page 44 also shows clearly where the various thinking tools detailed in the following section are going to be used. To assist those teachers who have not worked with the grid before, an additional matrix has been included on page 43. This shows only verbs placed in the various boxes.

A new 56-grid matrix has been created to reflect the suggested additon of a new sub-level to Bloom's Taxonomy, Pre-Knowing (Pirozzo, 2004). You will find a copy of the 56-grid matrix on page 42. This matrix should be used in catering for the needs of children with learning difficulties, ESL students and K-1 children who come from families where the language is not "elaborate".

Building the foundation

Promoting Learning International (48-grid) planning matrix

Unit of study: _____ **Year level:** _____

Eight ways to be smart	Bloom's taxonomy: Six thinking levels					
	Knowing	Understanding	Applying	Analysing	Creating	Evaluating
Verbal–linguistic I enjoy reading, writing and speaking						
Logical–mathematical I enjoy working with numbers and science						
Visual–spatial I enjoy painting, drawing and visualising						
Bodily–kinesthetic I enjoy doing hands-on activities, sports and dance						
Musical–rhythmic I enjoy making and listening to music						
Interpersonal–social I enjoy working with others						
Intrapersonal–intuitive I enjoy working by myself						
Naturalist I enjoy caring for plants and animals						

Promoting Learning International (56-grid) planning matrix

Unit of study: _____ **Year level:** _____

Bloom's taxonomy: Six thinking levels							
	Pre-Knowing	Knowing	Understanding	Applying	Analysing	Creating	Evaluating
Verbal–linguistic I enjoy reading, writing and speaking							
Logical–mathematical I enjoy working with numbers and science							
Visual–spatial I enjoy painting, drawing and visualising							
Bodily–kinesthetic I enjoy doing hands-on activities, sports and dance							
Musical–rhythmic I enjoy making and listening to music							
Interpersonal–social I enjoy working with others							
Intrapersonal–intuitive I enjoy working by myself							
Naturalist I enjoy caring for plants and animals							

Building the foundation

Promoting Learning International (48-grid) planning matrix

Unit of study: _____ **Year level:** _____

Eight ways to be smart	Bloom's taxonomy: Six thinking levels					
	Knowing	Understanding	Applying	Analysing	Creating	Evaluating
Verbal–linguistic I enjoy reading, writing and speaking	list	explain	report	investigate	create	argue
Logical–mathematical I enjoy working with numbers and science	find	convert	calculate	arrange	devise	rate
Visual–spatial I enjoy painting, drawing and visualising	locate	draw	illustrate	compare and contrast	design	assess
Bodily–kinesthetic I enjoy doing hands-on activities, sports and dance	play	outline	show	separate	plan	recommend
Musical–rhythmic I enjoy making and listening to music	listen	interpret	record	analyse	compose	judge
Interpersonal–social I enjoy working with others	relate	share	construct	survey	reflect	debate
Intrapersonal–intuitive I enjoy working by myself	state	describe	examine	identify	imagine	self evaluate
Naturalist I enjoy caring for plants and animals	name	express	classify	select	research	decide

Promoting Learning International (48-grid) planning matrix

Unit of study: _____ **Year level:** _____

Eight ways to be smart	Bloom's taxonomy: Six thinking levels					
	Knowing	Understanding	Applying	Analysing	Creating	Evaluating
Verbal–linguistic I enjoy reading, writing and speaking	list all the people in the story	explain how you will … **(WINCE)**	make a poster for … **(LDC)**	analyse a letter to the … **(BROW)**	create a new cover for …	review the …
Logical–mathematical I enjoy working with numbers and science	write the formula for the following …	match the plants and animals in the …	solve this problem **(Trec)**	investigate how a potato floats **(PSDR)**	devise an experiment **(SCRAM)**	justify why this law should be …
Visual–spatial I enjoy painting, drawing and visualising	look at all the paintings relating to …	draw pictures about …	illustrate a book titled …	use a **Venn diagram** to compare	design a model of … **(TAP)**	prepare guidelines to …
Bodily–kinesthetic I enjoy doing hands-on activities, sports and dance	name all the sports played in …	describe the movements of the girl in …	plan a physical education lesson	use the **W chart** to select …	create and perform a play dealing with …	critique a dance and suggest improvements
Musical–rhythmic I enjoy making and listening to music	listen to a number of …	explain songs dealing with …	classify this music **(LDC)**	how does this music compare to	compose a rhythm **(TAP)**	review a musical and suggest …
Interpersonal–social I enjoy working with others	tell about your project **(TPSS)**	outline the issues dealing with …	prepare a group discussion	interview a movie star **(Y chart)**	conduct an **X chart** on …	assess & recommend changes to …
Intrapersonal–intuitive I enjoy working by myself	state how you felt when …	visualise that you are at … **(The rake)**	show how you reacted to … **(A&R)**	arrange your own … **(CM, MM)**	predict what will happen if … **(ARC)**	use **SOWC** to advise changes to …
Naturalist I enjoy caring for plants and animals	locate all the tropical rainforests	how do you feel when you see … **(X or Y chart)**	organise a collection of insects	identify the best ways to save the …	devise an efficient way to compost **(WINCE)**	should we drill for oil in the … **(SOWC)**

Applying the knowledge

Using tools for improving thinking

Thinking tools are the strategies or scaffolding through which students can access the curriculum. They can be defined as artificial devices that have been developed specifically to improve thinking by:

- focusing (visually) their attention to an issue that needs to be resolved
- getting immediate feedback by seeing their ideas on paper
- providing a framework to organise ideas and data
- seeing the big picture
- making new connections
- analysing complex situations
- explaining relationships between concepts
- developing new thinking skills
- producing a larger number of possible solutions
- making informed choices
- constructing new knowledge
- creating new ideas and products.

Thinking tools are not new. In fact, Edward de Bono has been promoting the direct teaching of thinking skills since the early seventies through his Cognitive Research Trust (CoRT) and by his pioneering lateral thinking.

What is new and exciting is the fact that the 48 and 56-grid matrix provides a framework that enables you to direct students to use the most appropriate thinking tools to solve an issue or a problem. Embedding thinking tools into the matrix of activities can assist students to complete the activity as shown in the framework of the thinking classroom.

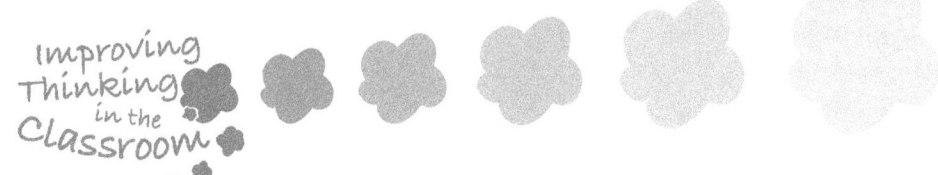

The thinking tool kit

The thinking tool kit contains tools that can be used by students as strategies to expand their thinking.

Name of tool	Acronyms	Page
A&R	Action and reaction	69
ARC	Action, reaction, consequences	69
BROW	Brainstorm, read, organise, write	62
Concept maps	Visual organisers that promote convergent thinking	57
LDC	Like, dislike, challenging	55
Mind maps	Visual organisers that promote divergent thinking	59
PSDR	Predict, share, do, reflect	60
SCRAM	Substitute, create, rewrite, audition, modify	68
SOWC analysis	Strengths, opportunities, weaknesses, consequences	66
TAP	Think all possibilities	56
The Rake	Touch, smell, taste, look, listen	53
TREC	Think, read, estimate, calulate	63
Venn diagrams	Compare and contrast	64
W chart	Look, sound, feel, taste, think	51
WINCE	Want, identify, need, create, evaluate	61
X chart	Look, sound, feel, think	49
Y chart	Look, sound, feel	47

Applying the knowledge

Y chart

Description
The Y chart is a descriptive tool describing what something looks like, feels likes and sounds likes. The Y chart provides students with a visual framework on which to gather and write all their thoughts.

Thinking skills
Describing, understanding, classifying, organising.

Scenario
The children are stranded in the jungle. Ask them to record what they would see, hear and feel in the jungle.

- Organise class into working groups of three or four students
- Provide each group with large sheets of butcher's paper and three different coloured textas.
- Once students have their ideas recorded, it becomes a much easier task to write a letter or a diary account of their adventure. Key words are identified and the range of ideas provides more stimulus for them.

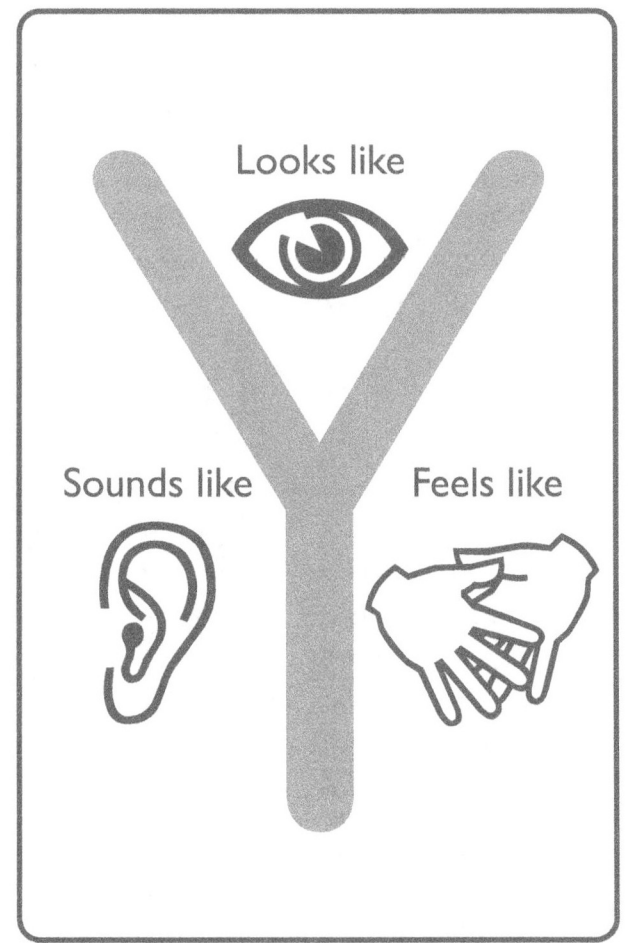

Variations
Let students select the choice of place where they are stranded and then let everyone try to guess where the place is from the clues in the Y chart.

This activity can also be used to describe objects.

Example: Y chart

Looks like

monkeys, birds and lizards
green colours everywhere
lots of scary creatures
wet and damp ground
snakes, frogs, spiders
Will we see Tarzan?
spooky and scary
dark and misty
tangled trees
huge canopy
torn clothes
cold

Sounds like

raindrops falling
lots of growling sounds
eerie sounds
birds chirping
snakes hissing
owls hooting
lions growling
squealing monkeys
croaking frogs
slithering snakes
crawling insects
whistling wind
rustling noises
ground shaking

Feels like

scared and frightened
insecure and worried
alone and dehydrated
wet and cold
I'm hungry … Where is Mum?
mosquitoes biting you
I need a shower
things brushing against you
tiny, tired, thirsty
you're going to lose the plot
scary eyes are watching me
angry, sad, lonely, crying
I'm busting – I need a toilet!
It's so hot – I'm suffocating!

Applying the knowledge

X chart

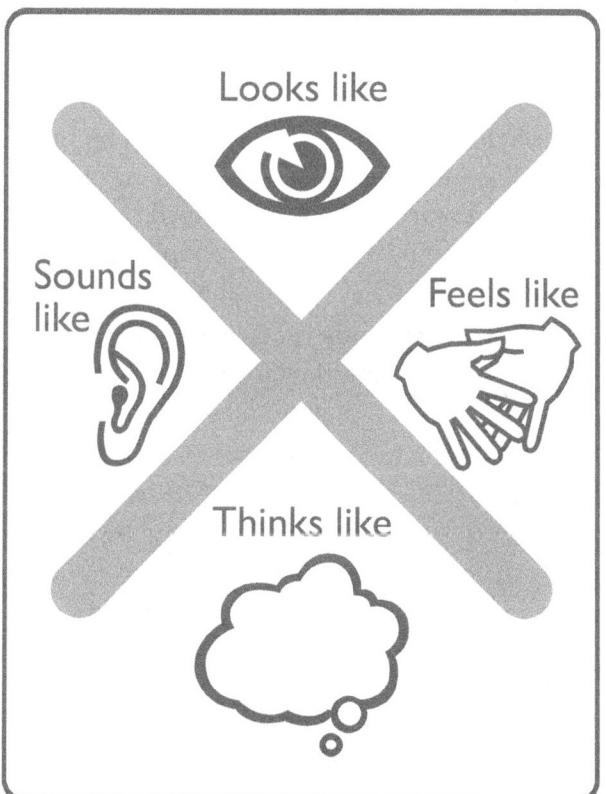

Description

The X chart is similar to the Y chart but provides an extra dimension. The X chart adds thoughts as the fourth dimension. Students can record their ideas about what they see, feel, hear and *think*. This is particularly important for adding an affective aspect to the scenario.

Thinking skills

Describing, classifying, explaining, organising, inferring.

Scenario

A group of children are bullying you in the playground. Record what you would see hear, feel and think on such an occasion.

- Brainstorm the ideas as a class.
- Record all ideas on the whiteboard.

Once this has been completed ask the children to write a story about someone being bullied. Have them include at least 5* words from each section of the chart.

*The number of words can be varied depending on the age of the students.

Example: X chart

Looks like
angry faces
insecure/scared
small/vulnerable
oppressed/worthless
hunched shoulders
mean/angry
withdrawn
following me
pulling faces
crowd building up
people rushing in
being surrounded
Everybody is staring at me
pointing/pushing
long/sad face
punching
defenceless
crying

Sounds like
loud sobbing
arguing
slamming
screaming
threatening
taunting
intimidating
harsh voices
foul language
negative messages
nah nah
name calling
leave me alone
cheering/booing
whispering
ridiculing
swearing
yelling
laughing
teasing

Feels like
fear/terror
doesn't exist
scared/sad
depressed/suicidal
misunderstood
picked on
insignificant
afraid/hurt
cornered
helpless
embarrassed
sickening
intimidated
frightened
powerless
singled out
isolated
victimised
ashamed
trapped
lonely
loser

Thinks like
unfair – why me?
How can I stop this?
How can I get away?
I've had enough – I can't go on
What am I supposed to do?
No-one knows what it's like
I don't want to come to school tomorrow
I hate myself and them   I have no friends
How can I escape?   I am a failure
How do I survive?   I don't want to be here
Where am I safe?   I can't tell anyone
Who can help?   What have I done?
Everybody hates me   I am worthless
I can't win   Not my fault
What's wrong with me?   No-one likes me

Applying the knowledge

W chart

Looks like	Feels like	Sounds like	Tastes like	Thinks like

Description
The W chart has five aspects – what you see, hear, feel, think and *taste*. This is particularly important in describing food.

Thinking skills
Describing, classifying, explaining, organising, inferring.

Scenario
Present a role-play to describe the best or the worst meal you have ever eaten.

Divide the students into groups of 3–4. Have each group complete the following questions in the chart:

- How did you feel when you were eating the meal?
- How did the food look?
- How did the meal taste?
- What sounds did you hear? What were people saying?
- What thoughts went through your mind?

Have each group practise their role-play before presenting to the class.

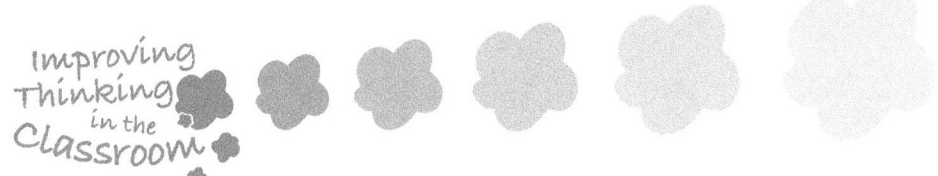

Example: W chart

Thinks like
Another family BBQ …
How much longer will they all stay?
I wonder what my friends are doing?
Why are BBQ sausages always black?
How many sausages will the average Australian eat in a lifetime?

Tastes like
bread and butter
mum's yucky coleslaw
caramelised onions
sausages/rissoles
tomato sauce
charcoal

Sounds like
sizzling food
mum laughing
tongs clinking
kids yelling
dad yelling
glasses chinking

Feels like
slapping mosquitoes
sticky lemonade
swatting flies
prickly grass
humid
hot

Looks like
outside
dad cooking
smoke/flames
burnt sausages
burnt rissoles
burnt onions

Applying the knowledge

The Rake

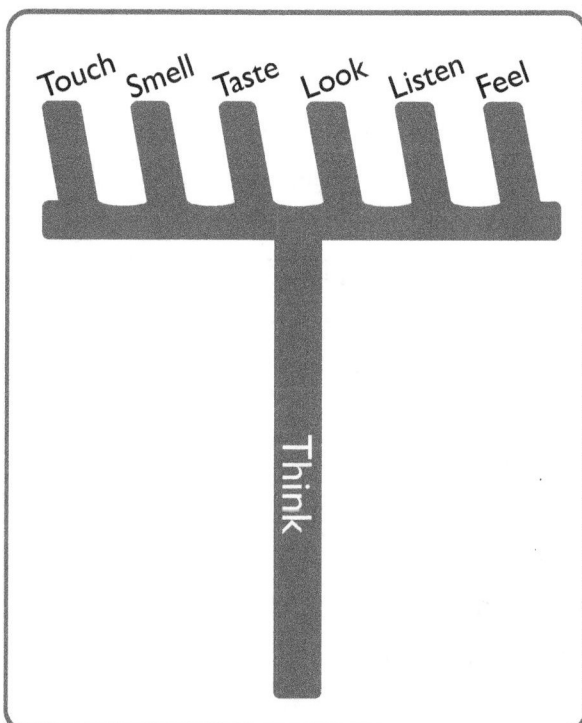

Description
The Rake has seven aspects – one each for touch, smell, taste, sight, hearing, feelings (emotions) and thinking.

Thinking skills
Describing, classifying, explaining, organising, inferring, fluency.

Scenario
You are visiting Antarctica and you find that you have lost your group. Describe your experience and then write a letter to your parents or a friend sharing with them how you have survived in Antartica.

The Rake

Touch	Smell	Taste	Look	Listen	Think	Feel

Whilst moving around your new 'place', list the following.

Choosing the right tool

Knowing the tools is important but understanding when to use them is even more important. To give children practice in which tools are best to use, choose one of the scenarios and encourage the children to complete it by selecting the best thinking tool they need.

Other activities for using with the X, Y & W charts and the Rake	Thinking tool
You have just come face to face with T-Rex!	
As you open the door, you notice that a burglar has come into your room by breaking the window.	
Whilst shopping you see your best friend stealing a pair of sunglasses.	
A group of children are bullying you in the playground.	
Your grandmother has just won a million dollars.	
You are entering the class after a two-week suspension.	
Your parents accuse you of staining their brand new carpet.	
Imagine that one day while you are out swimming a white pointer shark attacks you.	
Your parents tell you 'It is your fault that your brother was hit by the car whilst he was crossing the road.'	
Your grandparents have bought you your first puppy/kitten for your birthday.	
A lady is on the telephone saying that your family has won a trip to Disneyland.	
Your class is going on camp for a week and you have been told that you cannot go.	
There is a knock on the door. It is the social worker to take you to the juvenile detention centre.	
You have been grounded for the next two weeks.	
Your best friend has come first in the maths competition.	
As you enter the stage you cannot remember your lines.	
You have been working at it for a week and you finally get the right answer.	
You have been chosen to represent your school at your favourite sport.	

After they have filled in the chart, discuss the choices they have made, asking them to justify their selection.

Applying the knowledge

LDC
Like/Dislike/Challenging

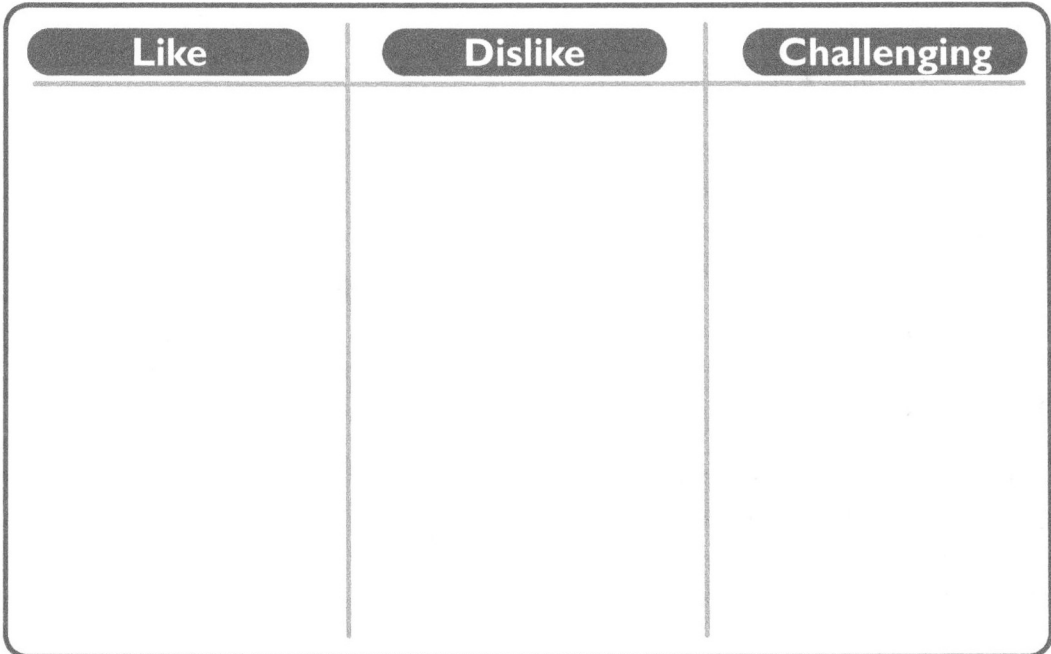

Description

The LDC is a reflective thinking tool that can be used in three ways: self-assessment, teacher assessment and peer assessment. This tool encourages children to reflect on their work and to receive feedback from their teachers and peers in a safe and structured manner.

The L stands for 'like' and this represents good things about an idea or a thing. The D, for 'dislike', lists the negative aspects. The C refers to those aspects of an idea or thing that are 'challenging' or that can be modified.

Thinking skills

Analysis, judgement, explanation.

Scenario

Prepare a poster of a plant eating dinosaur and then present your work to the class. Now, invite the other students to provide you feedback by using the LDC.

I like …
I dislike …
I found … challenging.

TAP
Think all possibilities

Description
The TAP is an inquiry based thinking tool. For example, it encourages children to brainstorm different ways to design a cover page for their reports or to empathise with a person/character.

This thinking tool has been designed to encourage children to brainstorm as many ideas as possible. It can also be used to encourage students to brainstorm different points of view and how different individuals feel about the same issue.

Thinking skills
Analysis, flexibility, fluency.

Scenario
There has been a suggestion that the school day should be longer – starting at 8:00 a.m. and finishing at 5:00 p.m. This would ensure children were safe and appropriately supervised, and it would help the increasing number of homes where two parents are working. People think it could be used to encourage fitness and outdoor activities and ensure homework is completed.

1. Organise children into groups and let them choose one of the following roles. The roles will help students think of different possibilities.

student	teacher	principal
parent/guardian	grandparents	public transport officials

2. Allow students 5–10 minutes to prepare themselves for their roles.

3. Encourage each student to share their ideas and responses to the issue.

4. Carry out a class debate or discussion.

5. Review with the class how this strategy helped them to deepen their thinking.

Applying the knowledge

Concept maps

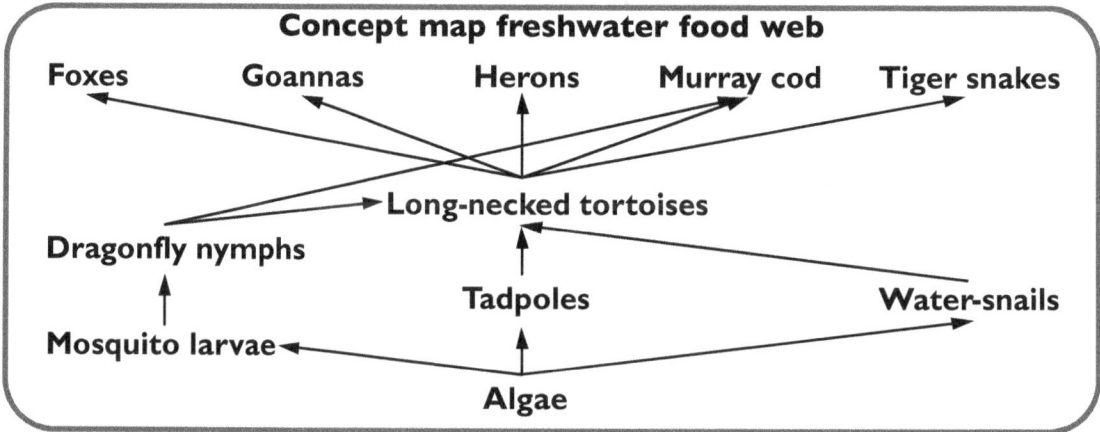

Description
Concept maps are extremely useful in enabling students to see the 'big picture' and to organise data by discovering relationships between various concepts. Because concept maps lead the brain to begin in one area and then proceed through a logical and sequential framework, they often tend to favour convergent learners.

Thinking skills
Analysing, classifying, organising, structuring, ordering.

Scenario
Create you own food web.

Instructions
- Cut each food web card out.
- Organise these in a way that makes sense to you.
- Glue the plants and animals onto butcher's paper.
- Connect each plant/animal with a straight line.
- Place an arrow at the end of each line to indicate that this animal is going to eat the animal or plant below it.
- Write *eaten by* on each line.
- Further activities
    - Find pictures and place them on the foodweb.
    - Research what algae eat.
    - Colour code water, land and flying animals in different colours.
    - Choose one of the animals and compose a song, mime, rap or play.
    - Explain why the algae are the essential component on the food web.
    - What will happen if the farmer sprays a herbicide?
    - Use percussion instruments to make the sounds of each animals.
    - Role-play the various animals in the food web.
    - Make a song starting with 'there was an old man/woman …'
    - Act out your favourite animal in the food web.

Food web cards

Fox	Tiger snake
Heron	Goanna
Long-necked Tortoises	Murray cod
Dragonfly nymphs	Mosquito larvae
Tadpoles	Water snails
Algae	Tadpoles

Applying the knowledge

Thinking clouds

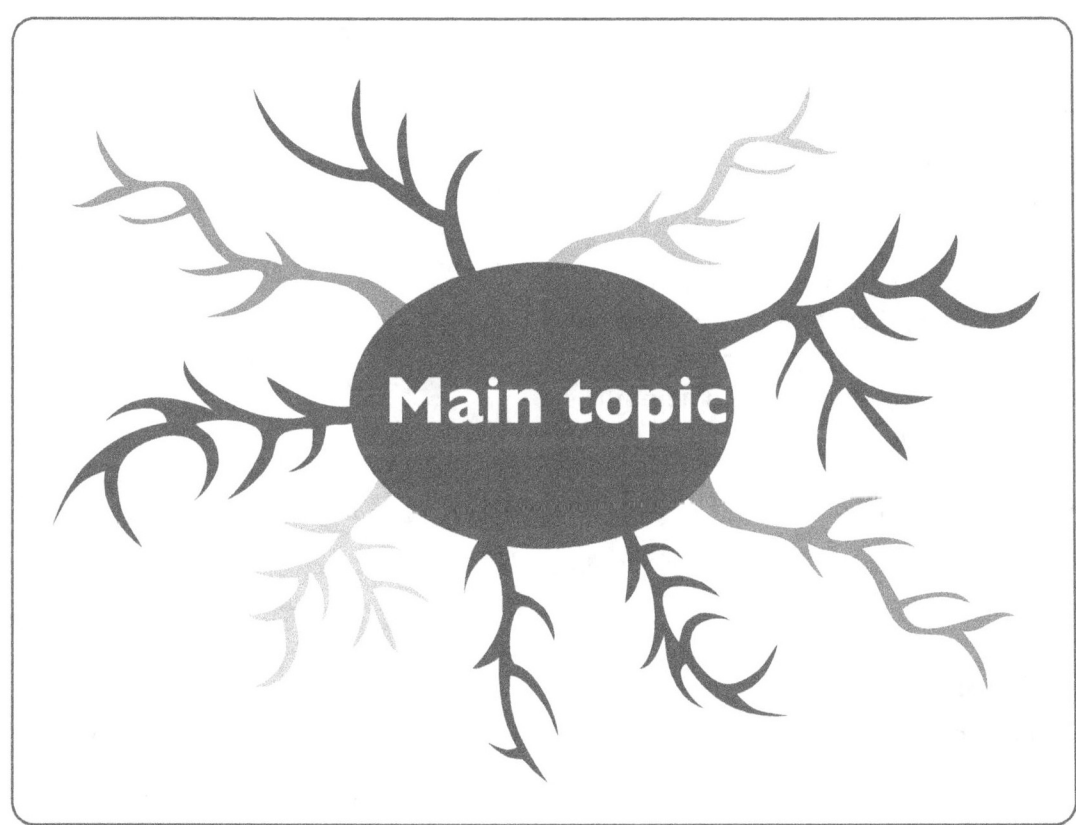

Description

Thinking clouds are used to represent your thinking as a map, which is a brain friendly way to follow your thoughts. Thinking clouds can be used to represent already written text, or to brainstorm ideas about a central theme or topic.

Thinking clouds promote divergent thinking. They encourage us to dream, to brainstorm and be highly imaginative and creative. Thinking Clouds have been based on the work of Tony Buzan and Nancy Marguiles, are fun interactive way to get ideas onto paper. Since 2003, the author has found that young children react very favourably to the term Thinking Clouds.

Thinking Skills

Creating, fluency, flexibility, organising.

Scenario

Brainstorm all the places in the world where you could get 'lost' and then write and/or draw this information on your mind map. You need to include at least 10 entries.

PSDR

Predict/Share/Do/Reflect

Description
The PSDR encourages students to go through a four stage thinking process that involves:
- predicting what will happen when …
- sharing their thoughts with others
- doing the experiment
- reflecting on the outcome of the experiment.

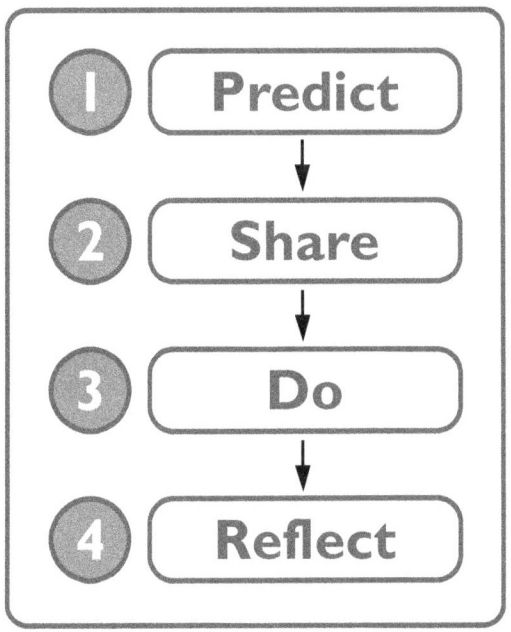

Thinking skills
Predicting, inferring, hypothesising, applying, reflecting.

Scenario
Floating potatoes

Prepare two similar buckets as follows: both buckets contain the same amount of water (approximately 3.5 litres). However, bucket A has fresh water, while bucket B has about 800 g of salt dissolved in it.

1. **Predict**
   What will happen when the potato is placed in each bucket?
   Suggestions may include:
   - the potato will pop out of the water
   - the potato will float/sink
   - water will get inside the potato and it will explode
   - nothing will happen.
2. **Share**
   Share with your partner why you have made this prediction.
3. **Experiment**
   Place the potato in bucket A. Observe what happens.
   Place the potato in the bucket B. Observe the results.
4. **Reflect**
   Explain the difference in the result.

Applying the knowledge

WINCE
Want/Identify/Need/Create/Evaluate

Want	Identify	Need	Create	Evaluate
What do I **want** to know?	**Identify** what I already know?	What additional information do I **need**?	What have I **created**?	What have I learned from **evaluating** this activity?

Description

The WINCE strategy is a five-stage problem-solving process.
- **W**hat children would like to know
- **I**dentify the challenge or problem to be solved
- deciding on extra information they may **N**eed to find out
- **C**reating a solution
- **E**valuating what they have learned.

Thinking skills

Problem-solving, analysing, creating, evaluating.

Scenario

Make a potato float halfway up the bucket of water, without using any weights and/or strings and by keeping the level of the water at 2 cm below the lid.

- One way of achieving this is to use the information that the children have gathered by carrying out the potato experiment using the PSDR Method.

- However, the children will need an additional bucket which will be referred to as bucket C. This bucket is the same size as buckets A and B. Pour enough salty water from bucket B into C until it is half full. The potato now floats in the middle of the bucket. Then, enough ice cubes are added until the water level reaches 2 cm below the lid whilst the potato floats in the middle of the bucket.

- It is essential that the chidren now evaluate what they have learned and investigate other ways that this could be achieved.

BROW

Brainstorm/Review/Organise/Write

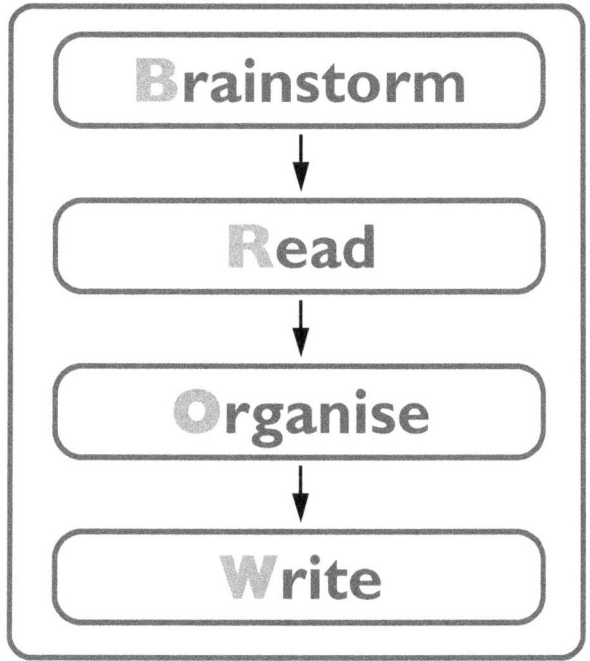

Description

In using BROW the children go through a four stage process
- **B**rainstorming
- **R**eading and reviewing
- **O**rganising
- **W**riting

Thinking skills

Fluency, flexibility, originality, problem-solving, organising.

Scenario

You have been chosen to design a marketing campaign for a new boat. You will need to prepare a single page advertisement for the boat. The advertisement may be for a newspaper, magazine or a website.

- Brainstorm all the different techniques that are used in advertising.

- Read and review other advertisements for new boats. Add to your list the important things these advertisements mention and the techniques used.

- Organise your information, pictures and words for your own advertisement.

- Write and produce your advertisement.

Applying the knowledge

TREC

Think/Read/Estimate/Calculate

Think	Read	Estimate	Calculate
Get your brain into action. When working with mathematics, what do we normally do?	Read the question. If you do not understand it, read it again. Ask your teacher for assistance.	Estimate what you believe the answer should be. Is your estimate similar to your team members?	Carry out the calculations required. How close is your answer to your estimation? How do you know that you have the right answer?

Description

TREC involves children in a four stage framework that directs children to:

- **T**hink about numbers
- **R**ead and discuss the problem to be solved until they understand what is involved in the task
- **E**stimate what the cost of building the boat is likely to be
- **C**alculate answers.

TREC is particularly useful to scaffold children into doing maths. This tool ensures that students know what they need to do by encouraging them to go through a four stage approach. One of the critical stages is for the children to understand the problem that they have to solve. Thus, TREC encourages the children to read the question and if they still don't understand it to read it again, then to discuss it with their group and finally to ask their teacher for assistance.

Thinking skills

Recalling, interpreting, estimating, evaluating.

Scenario

You are the accountant in a small boat building business. The designers have come up with a new design (from a previous activity) and you have been asked to provide a cost for building the boat.

Use TREC to help you do the costing.
- Think about numbers.
- Read the way the boat is going to be built and what will need to be included in the costs (e.g. materials and labour).
- Estimate what the cost of building the boat is likely to be.
- Carry out the required calculations.

Venn diagrams
Compare & contrast

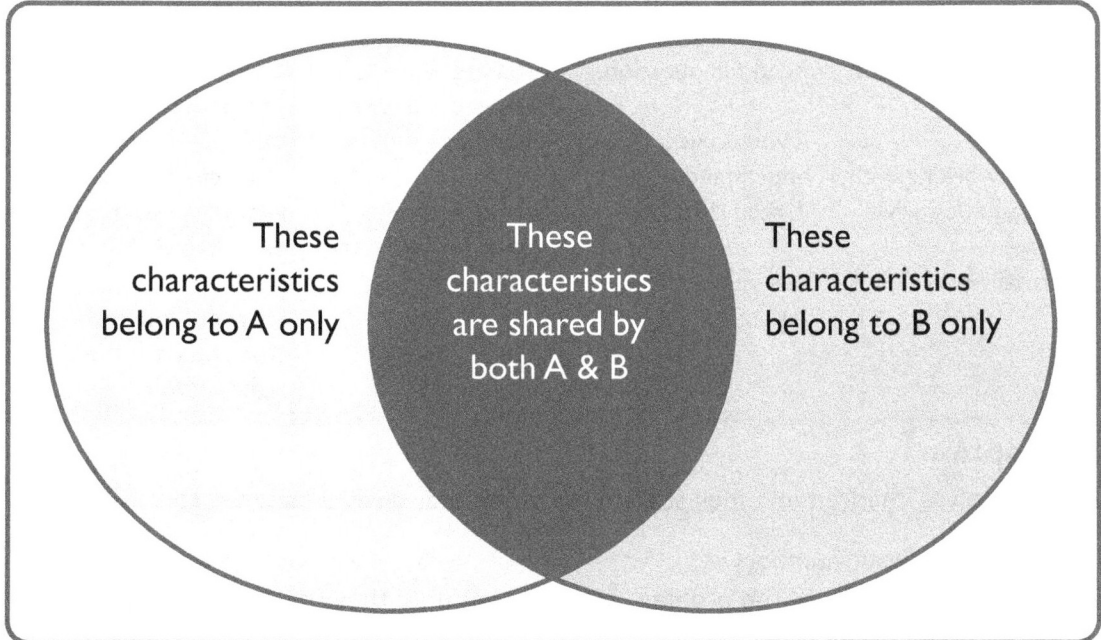

Description
The Venn diagram was designed by John Venn (1834–1923) and has been used by teachers for many years. This is the author's interpretation of Venn diagrams.

Application
Recalling, comparing, contrasting.

Scenario
Your grandparents are moving to a retirement village where space is extremely limited. However, they love animals and are determined to take one pet with them. Their preferred animals are dogs and cats.

Students with well developed logical–mathematical and visual–spatial intelligence could now decide whether a dog or a cat should be taken by their grandparents to the retirement village by using the Venn diagram (see example p. 65).

Based on the results of the Venn diagram, which animal did the children suggest that their grandparents take to the retirement village and why?

Applying the knowledge

Example: Venn diagram

DOGS
Smooth tongue
Bark
Canine
Short wiskers
Omnivore
Swim in water
No claws
Train easily
Some dribble
Need more attention
Don't climb
Well domesticated

Pets
Mammals
Live babies
Hair and fur
Whiskers
Eat meat
Domesticated

CATS
Meow, purr
Rough tongue
Feline
Long whiskers
Partially domesticated
Climb
Bury faeces
Retractable claws
Sharp claws
Groom themselves
Need less attention
Don't train easily

Now, the children can choose any of the following and list the differences and similarities in a Venn diagram

Compare and contrast	
Telephone	Mobile phones
Day	Night
Winter	Summer
Evil	Good
Democracy	Dictatorship
Leader	Follower
Friend	Enemy
Old	New
Dishonest	Honest

SOWC analysis
Strengths/Opportunities/ Weaknesses /Consequences
Level 1

Strengths	Opportunities	Weaknesses	Consequences

Description
SOWC level 1
Level 1 requires students to brainstorm strengths, opportunities, weaknesses and consequences of an idea, or an issue. However, it does not solve the issue/problem being discussed. For that the students should analyse and prioritise their data through SOWC analysis level 2 and then become personally involved through SOWC analysis level 3.

SOWC level 2
Having completed SOWC analysis level 1 students now analyse the data, prioritise the most important issues and transfer this data to SOWC analysis level 2.

A maximum of five or six critical issues should appear on each quadrant of SOWC analysis level 2. Whilst working at this level, can the students:
- match strengths to weaknesses
- convert weaknesses to strengths
- convert consequences to opportunities.

The students should now be able to state clearly what they are going to do to solve this problem.

SOWC level 3
The students are now ready to move onto SOWC analysis level 3.
- What are the activities they are going to undertake?
- How are they going to complete these activities?
- Who is going to do what?
- When is this going to happen?
- Will there be any cost involved?

Note: SOWC is the author's interpretation of the old SWOT.

Applying the knowledge

Level 2

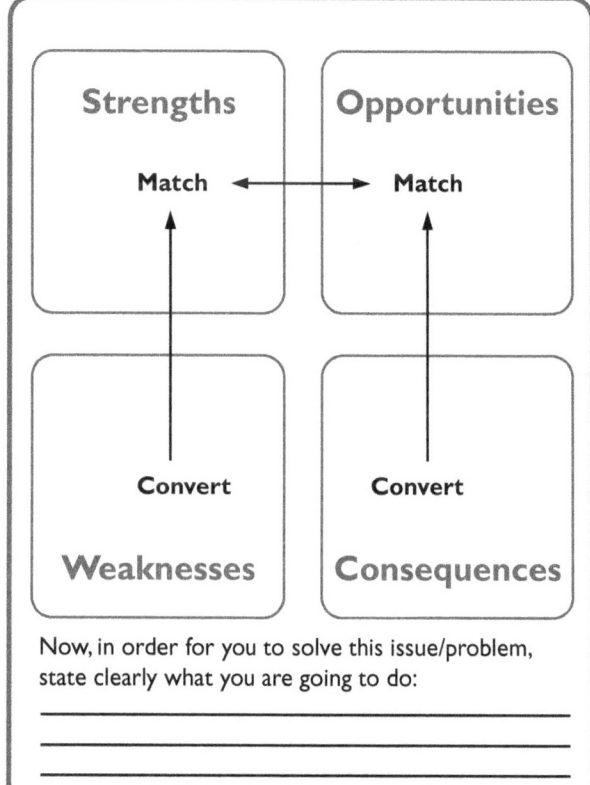

Now, in order for you to solve this issue/problem, state clearly what you are going to do:
_____
_____
_____

Thinking skills
Problem-solving.

Scenario
Should space exploration continue?

Use SOWC to analyse this controversial issue and to make the relevant recommendations.

Other topics for SOWC analysis
Why have rules in our classroom?
How can we deal effectively with bullying?
Should we drill for gas or oil on the Great Barrier Reef?
What would happen if we did not wear uniforms?
The year is 2020: Predict the effects of genetic engineering.
Should we set up separate classes for boys and girls?
Which secondary school will you choose?
Should we keep children in detention centres?
Your parents are planning to move to a large city or a small town. Will you be in favour of this move? How will you decide?

Level 3
What will you do to solve this problem?

What?	How?	Who?	When?	Costs?

SCRAM

Substitute/Combine/Rate/ Adapt/Modify

Possible verbs that can be used with this strategy are:

S	**C**	**R**	**A**	**M**
Substitute	**C**ombine	**R**ate	**A**dapt	**M**odify
Separate	**C**lassify	**R**eport	**A**ct	**M**agnify
Solve	**C**ompare	**R**esearch	**A**dvise	**M**ake
Suggest	**C**omplete	**R**estate	**A**nalyse	**M**ime
Survey	**C**ompose	**R**eview	**A**pply	**M**inimise
	Conduct	**R**ewrite	**A**rgue	
	Construct		**A**rrange	
	Contrast		**A**ssess	
	Create		**A**udition	

Description

SCRAM is one of the most versatile thinking tools because different verbs can be selected from each of the five columns depending on the activity that the children are involved in. For example:

Substitute   **C**reate   **R**ewrite   **A**udition   **M**odify

Thinking skills

Creating, evaluating.

Scenario

Write a new version of the story of the three little pigs.

- Substitute a ferocious lion for one of the little pigs.
- Create a story/poem/play dealing with the story of a bully in your school.
- Little pigs are not able to climb trees. Now rewrite the story.
- Use the Rake or the X, Y & W charts to audition for the role of the little pig that lives in the house made of bricks.
- The little pig and the wolf live in Cairns, north Queensland, where there is no need to have chimneys. How would this have changed the story?

Applying the knowledge

A&R and ARC
Action & Reaction
Action/Reaction/Consequences

Action	Reaction
What will you do now?	How will the other person react?

Description
The A&R and the ARC are thinking tools that will help children to empathise with another person and to make informed decisions. However, the A&R strategy is best suited to younger children.

Thinking skills
Reflecting, empathising, decision making

Scenario
In completing the integrated project titled 'Out in space' the children need to build a space station whose workforce is made up of:
- Manager
- Five children
- Doctor/dentist

- Nurse
- Two supervisors
- 40 workers

A great deal of time, energy and money has been spent in ensuring that all the individuals chosen work well together. Human nature being what it is, it's hard to imagine that there will be no conflict when a large number of individuals are asked to work together in such a restricted environment.

Using their interpersonal–social and visual–spatial intelligences students could use the A&R and ARC to solve the following conflicts.

1. While an experienced worker is completing a job on the space station, the supervisor comes over and says in a most intimidating manner, 'What are you doing? Can't you see that this is completely wrong?'

2. How should the worker reply to the supervisor? (Use A&R to frame your answer.)

3. After just two weeks on the space station one of the workers finds that they don't share any of the team's values, interests or hobbies and has lost all interest in the project.

Have the students role-play this scenario by working through the three stages involved in the ARC. The aim of this should be to show the worker that for any action taken there will be a reaction from the other team members, their supervisors and the manager. Undeniably, there will also be consequences.

ARC

Action	Reaction	Consequences
What will you do now?	How will the other person react?	What will be the outcomes?

Applying the knowledge

Choosing the right tool

Knowing the tools is important, but understanding when to use them is even more so. To give students practice in deciding which tools are best to use, choose one of the scenarios from the table below and/or on the following page and encourage them to complete it by selecting the best thinking tool to use in solving the problem. In some tasks several tools may be used consecutively to solve a problem.

Other activities using A&R/ARC, BROW, concept maps, LDC, mind maps, PSDR, SCRAM, SOWC analysis, TAP, TREC, Venn diagrams or WINCE	Thinking tool
Write a rap song about your new country.	
You have just returned from your school camp. On the camp you tried many different activities. Write a report on the activities and how you felt about each of them.	
If you were prime minister what would you change about your country?	
Write a Top Five Holiday Destinations list for each member of your family.	
Calculate how much it would cost to redecorate your room.	
You have been chosen for an Australian Junior sports team. How might other people feel about this?	
Design and carry out an experiment to see whether plants need light?	
Design a new piece of jewellery. It should be original – it should be something that is new and different.	
The Education Department has decided that the only drink allowed in schools is water. No other drinks can be brought from home or sold in the tuckshop or canteen. What effect would this decision have?	
Write a report on the varieties of dinosaurs that have been discovered. Show the locations of where each type of dinosaur has been found.	
Show the structure of the Australian government.	
Write a one page essay on Sport.	
Describe the ecosystem of the rainforest.	
Design a new form of single person transport.	
Rewrite your own version of the three little pigs.	
Every year the school has a billycart race and as this is your last year at the school you would really like to win. Make your plans.	

Continued on page 72

Choosing the right tool (cont.)

Other activities using A&R/ARC, BROW, concept maps, LDC, mind maps, PSDR, SCRAM, SOWC analysis, TAP, TREC, Venn diagrams or WINCE	Thinking tool
How good are you at completing homework? Evaluate your performance.	
Prepare a debate on Euthanasia.	
What would happen if you tried to grow plants in a box with the top covered in green cellophane. The box has holes for air to circulate. Would this increase the growth of the plant?	
How can we deal effectively with bullying?	
Should there be separate classes for girls and boys?	
Use a diagram to explain the organisation of your school.	
Your parents are planning to move to a small city/large town and they have asked your opinion. What will you tell them?	
Your local council has decided to allow a world class theme park to be built in your neighbourhood. Write a report for or against the proposal.	
Debate whether animals should be used in experiments.	
It is planned to close your school. The nearest school is half an hour away. What effect will this have on you, the other students and your district?	
You have decided to start a crocodile/llama farm. Prepare a report on what you will need and what you will need to know to start the farm.	
You have been asked to read and summarise a report on human cloning.	
Compare the advantages of a holiday in Australia and a holiday in the United States of America.	
Your parents have given you permission to redecorate your room. But before they will allow you to go ahead they want to discuss your plans and the costs. Prepare your plans.	
Invent a new improved hairdryer.	
Should human cloning be allowed? Prepare a speech.	

After students have completed this chart, discuss the choices they have made, asking them to justify their selection.

Applying the knowledge

Transferring the knowledge to the real-world: 48 and 56-grid matrix

Real assessment tasks

In our search for a structure that enables teachers to anchor their thinking skills program and the engagement of their children, we have found that the 48 and 56-grid matrix is an outstanding framework. This combination of Bloom's taxonomy, multiple intelligences and the tools for thinking, is a useful and practical model that ensures depth and rigour and engagement in activities, lessons and units. In particular, the 48 and 56-grid matrix offers various pathways to scaffold students so that they will be able to successfully complete real assessment tasks.

Real assessment tasks, or integrated projects, have developed because life outside the classroom is rarely compartmentalised into neat little categories, and a growing number of students find what they learn at school is somewhat irrelevant to their lives. The underlying philosophy of an integrated project is to:

- Connect students to their learning by engaging them to apply their skills and knowledge to solve real-world problems.

- Encourage children to construct knowledge rather than being passive receivers of information.

- Integrate various subject areas in order to reduce the amount of similar material taught by different faculties.

- Rely on teamwork.

In deciding how a real assessment task should be structured, teachers need to understand **authentic pedagogy**, also known as productive pedagogies and quality teaching. Authentic pedagogy was first investigated by Fred Newmann and associates at the Center on Organisation and Restructuring of Schools (CORS) based at the University of Wisconsin.

The theory of quality teaching is based on the premise that students' work in the classroom should prepare them for the intellectual work that will be demanded of

them as adults (Newmann and Wehlage, 1995). Furthermore, Newmann and associates (1996) argued that authentic academic achievement can be defined through three criteria that are critical to significant intellectual accomplishments:

1. Construction of knowledge
2. Disciplined inquiry
3. Value beyond school.

Then, they developed the following seven standards for authentic achievement.

Standards for authentic pedagogy: Assessment tasks	
Construction of knowledge	**Standard 1: Organization of information** The task asks students to organize, synthesize, interpret, explain, or evaluate complex information in addressing a concept, problem, or issue.
	Standard 2: Consideration of alternatives The task asks students to consider alternative solutions, strategies, perspectives, or points of view in addressing a concept, problem, or issue.
Disciplined inquiry	**Standard 3: Disciplinary content** The task asks students to show understanding and/or to use ideas, theories, or perspectives considered central to an academic or professional discipline.
	Standard 4: Disciplinary process The task asks students to use methods of inquiry, research, or communication characteristic of an academic or professional discipline.
	Standard 5: Elaborated written communication The task asks students to elaborate on their understanding, explanations, or conclusions through extended writing.
Value beyond school	**Standard 6: Problem connected to the world beyond the classroom** The task asks students to address a concept, problem, or issue that is similar to one that they have encountered or are likely to encounter in life beyond the classroom.
	Standard 7: Audience beyond the school The task asks students to communicate their knowledge, present a product or performance, or take some action for an audience beyond the teacher, classroom, and school building.

Newmann, F.M. & associates (1996). *Authentic Achievement: Restructuring Schools for Intellectual Quality.* Jossey-Bass: San Francisco. This material is used by permission of John Wiley & Sons, Inc.

Transferring the knowledge to the real world

Core and elective

The matrix needs to have a clear structure rather than just being a collection of great activities. The foundation of this structure will be the assessment task that students need to work on in order to successfully complete the unit. Each matrix will have **core** and **elective** activities; there will also be a logical order in which the students will grow in their knowledge and understanding of the content.

By 'core', we refer to those activities that are so critical to the development of a concept that we will actually need to teach them to the students. Whereas, the 'electives' are those activities that students can learn on their own or by working in groups or accessing material from the Internet and from other different sources.

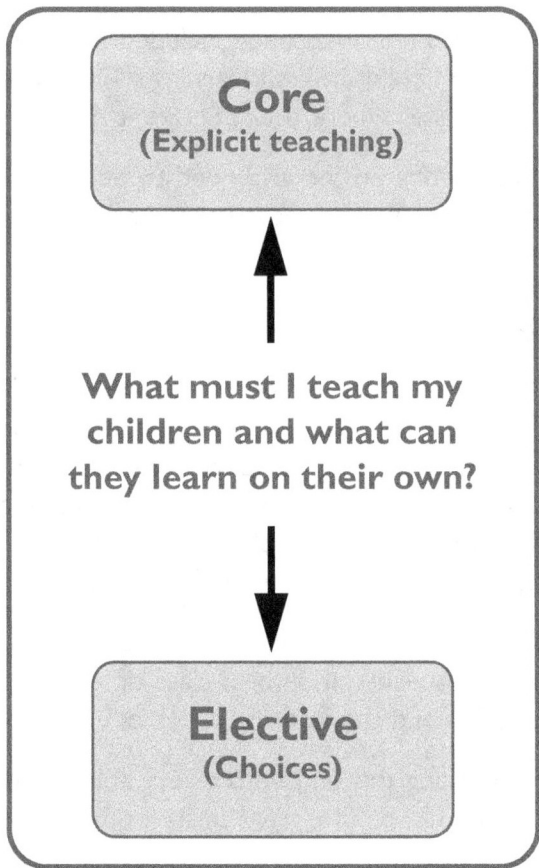

'Saving the koala' (pp. 78–79) was selected to show how the grid enables us to clearly identify the real assessment task, the thinking tools and the sequence that will be used to teach this unit. The matrix enables us to clearly state what we want our students to do, which is to prepare a well thought-out answer to the question, 'How will you prevent the Koala from becoming extinct?' The real assessment task becomes the beacon, or the purpose, for all the activities. Basically, this means that all the activities that we are going to do in this unit have one main goal: to scaffold the children so that they will be successful in completing their real assessment task.

In addition, the number assigned to each activity indicates the sequence used to teach this unit. This sequence can be changed and may differ greatly depending on the age, ability and behaviour of the children and the teacher's preferred teaching methods.

Unlike in the other examples, the core and elective activities on the 'Saving the Koala' grid have deliberately not been shaded. This means that the teachers teaching this unit will have the opportunity to choose which activities they will teach and which activities the children will be able to complete on their own, in groups or through learning centres or learning contracts.

In 'Out in space' (pp. 80–83) the shading shows core and elective activities enabling us to clearly identify where the assessment task, the thinking tools and the mandated learning outcomes are going to be placed.

The unit titled 'plants' (pp. 84–88) has been included to show how the 56-grid matrix caters for the needs of children with learning difficulties, ESL students and K–1 children who come from families where the language is not 'elaborate'.

Note that not all the activities on the grid need to be taught. Teachers will choose those activities that they believe will be most useful and appropriate to their children.

Learning outcomes

The matrix enables you to provide the students with a well-defined and authentic real assessment task. In the unit 'Out in space', students have to build a model of a factory in space. This factory will produce huge amounts of insulin needed by the large number of people that by 2020 will develop diabetes due to poor diet and insufficient physical exercise. The space station will employ 50 people who need to be looked after in terms of housing, food, clothing, exercises and entertainment.

There will be learning outcomes related to standards or essential learning that must be covered by all children. The amount of class time dedicated to these will depend entirely on the ability and the learning styles of each student.

Suppose that we are covering this unit with a very able group of children. It is most likely that they are not going to spend a great deal of time in revising basic understanding of place value, scales and measurement (e.g. mm, cm, m and km). On the other hand, if there are a number of children with learning difficulties then this will obviously be a very different story!

Scope and sequence

The numbering of the activities in the 48 and 56-grid matrix provides an effective and visual way of indicating the scope and sequence that will be used to teach a particular unit. This is very clearly illustrated in Example 1: 'Saving the koala' (pp. 78–79) and 'Case Study: Marketing your boat' (pp. 90–91). These numbers enable these activities

Transferring the knowledge to the real world

to be aligned with your department/school/college curriculum framework (eg. quality teaching and essential of learnings).

Preparing a 48 and 56-grid matrix

Here is a very useful and practical approach that seems to be working well in both primary and secondary schools:

1. Commence by identifying the relevant learning outcomes from the syllabus.

2. Specify the assessment task(s) that will enable our students to demonstrate the relevant learning outcomes.

3. Design an appropriate criteria/rubric that will be used to assess the assessment task(s).

4. Use the verbs from the Learning and teaching wheel (p. 14) to develop thinking skills (Depth).

5. Use the Engaging wheel (p. 37) and the Applying the engaging wheel (p. 38) to select those activities that will engage children through their preferred learning styles (Engagement).

6. Place the activities on the 48 and 56-grid matrix.

7. Shade the core, electives and assessment activities.

8. Highlight the thinking tools.

9. Select the most relevant cooperative learning strategies

10. Embed the learning outcomes on the grid.

11. Align the matrix with the quality teaching framework or the essentials of learning framework.

Many teachers have remarked that whilst planning these units it is an excellent idea to have available work programs, units of work, texts and copies of existing 48 and 56-grid matrix units.

Example 1: Saving the koala (Year level: 5–9)

Eight ways to be smart	Bloom's taxonomy: Six thinking levels	
	Knowing	Understanding
Verbal–linguistic I enjoy reading, writing and speaking	2. Carry out a **mind map** and then list all the known endangered species.	7. Explain why the whale has not become extinct.
Logical–mathematical I enjoy working with numbers and science	4. Visit <www.savethekoala.com> to find out how many koalas we have at present.	9. Use **Trec** to find out how much it will cost to prevent the koala from becoming extinct.
Visual–spatial I enjoy painting, drawing and visualising	1. Look at a number of posters and photographs of extinct animals that your teacher will bring to class.	5. Visit <www.savethekoala.com> Then, draw a map to show where most koalas live.
Body–kinesthetic I enjoy doing hands-on activities, sports and dance	10. Participate in a field trip to the local koala sanctuary and/or visit your local park.	13. Make cut-outs of your favourite endangered species.
Musical–rhythmic I enjoy making and listening to music	11. Learn a song dealing with saving an endangered species.	14. Choose a song about people caring for the environment and explain its meaning to your group.
Interpersonal–social I enjoy working with others	8. Should we keep animals in zoos? What is your personal opinion?	6. When is an animal endangered? Discuss this with your group.
Intrapersonal–intuitive I enjoy working by myself	29. What can your group do to stop a species from becoming extinct? Brainstorm using **TAP**.	22. Visualise yourself as an endangered species. How do you feel? Now complete the **Y chart**.
Naturalist I enjoy caring for plants and animals	3. What would your life be without plants and animals? **(TPSS)**	12. How do your feel when you see a koala that has been rescued from a car accident on TV?

Continued on page 79

Transferring the knowledge to the real world

Bloom's taxonomy: Six thinking levels			
Applying	Analysing	Creating	Evaluating
19. Using the **BROW** strategy, prepare a TV ad to protect the koala.	18. Why should we prevent species from becoming extinct?	**Real assessment task** How will you prevent the koala from becoming extinct? Your action plan will be presented to various groups including students, teachers, administrators, parents, local government officials and a number of environmental experts.	
23. Use the **TAP** strategy to brainstorm all the things that you can do to prevent the koala from becoming extinct.	24. Now, categorise the things that you can actually do to prevent the koala's extinction.		
16. Make a time line when dinosaurs were alive.	25. **Venn diagram**: koala and whales. What do they have in common?	41. Create your own web page dealing with 'Saving the koala'. Then, present it to your group and receive their feedback. You may choose the **LDC** tool as an evaluation strategy.	
17. Role play different endangered species. **(W chart)**	20. Arrange a poster for an endangered species.	34. Create and perform a play dealing with tree clearing.	36. Devise an environmental game that could be used to teach others.
42. Select music to be played whilst presenting your action plan to your group/class.	21. Pantomime koalas as they grow. **(The Rake)**	26. Compose a rhythm to save the koala.	37. Act and choreograph a dance about saving the koala's habitat.
33. Interview the manager of your local zoo.	31. Use **The Rake** and **TAP** to design a model of the 'best environment for the koala to live in'.		32. Present your 'best environment for the koala to live in' to your class. **(LDC)**
15. A day in the life of a young koala. Now, write a story to be published in the school newsletter and/or the local paper.	27. Share with your group your concerns about tree clearing. Identify how this can be stopped.	38. You are standing in front of a Koala whilst its 'home' is being destroyed. Now complete the **X chart**.	40. Assess whether the Koala will be extinct by the year 2020 by using the **SOWC analysis**.
28. How would you sell the idea of preserving an endangered species?	35. Analyse the things that you can do to become much more environmentally friendly.	30. Review the book 'Where the forest meets the sea'. Imagine you are the child in the book. **(Y chart)**	39. Determine the impact of tree removal on the survival of the koala.

Example 2: Out in space (Year level: 4–6)

Eight ways to be smart	Bloom's taxonomy: Six thinking levels	
	Knowing	Understanding
Verbal–linguistic I enjoy reading, writing and speaking	Read notes from the following sources: **The young astronomer** **100 Questions and Answers** **Astronomy Today** **The Collins Space Atlas** www.kids-space.org www.nasa.gov www.space.com www.ksc.nasa.gov	Define the following terms: comets, asteroids, planets, moons, gravity, space, solar system, moons, eclipses, astronomy, big bang theory
Logical–mathematical I enjoy working with numbers and science	Revise basic understanding of place value, scales and measurement (e.g. mm, cm, m and km). Of what value is the sun to us? Find out what determines night and day, and eclipses. How does the earth's atmosphere provide for our needs (e.g. air).	Why should we: study the solar system? Build space stations? How much will it cost to run your space station for a month/year? **(TREC)** How much insulin will the station have to produce to stay competitive? **(TREC)**
Visual–spatial I enjoy painting, drawing and visualising	Study various photographs of MIR and the International Space Station. How will you help the workers to know where they are in the space station?	Draw a rough draft of your space station. Is it to scale? Will you paint the floors and ceiling in different colours? Why?
Body–kinesthetic I enjoy doing hands-on activities, sports and dance	Look at a number of models of the solar system. Study photographs/videos of MIR and the International Space Station. What additional information will you need in order to build your own space station? **(WINCE)**	Explain what materials you will use in building your space station. Do you have experience in working with these materials? If the answer is NO, what will you do to gain this experience? Will you be doing any science experiments? If the answer is yes, do you have the proper equipment?

Continued on page 81

Transferring the knowledge to the real world

Bloom's taxonomy: Six thinking levels			
Applying	Analysing	Creating	Evaluating
Use the **BROW** strategy to enable you to commence writing your report. Make a rough 'draft' of your report/story script/drama production/video/play. Show your rough 'draft' to your teacher.	Review your teacher's comments and make whatever changes/ additions/deletions are necessary. Arrange your final report/story script/drama production/video/play to be presented to your class/school.	**Real assessment task** The year is 2020. Due to poor diet and insufficient physical exercise, many children are becoming obese and developing diabetes. The WDC* wants to build a factory in space to produce large amounts of insulin. Your job is to prepare a model of a space station that will employ 50 people. In addition, you will advise the WDC on how you will look after these workers in terms of housing, food, clothing, exercises and music. (*WDC: World Diabetes Council)	Present your story script/drama production/video/play to your class/school. Use the **LDC** strategy to encourage members of your class to provide you with their feedback.
In building your station, how will you look after your workers in terms of: clothing, food, sewage, oxygen, water, carbon dioxide, exercise, sleeping, electricity, social needs?	Investigate how you will prevent your workers from suffering: dizziness and nausea, muscle 'wastage', loss of calcium? Select different materials to take advantage of the sun's energy.		Carry out a debate titled 'Should space exploration continue?' **(SOWC Analysis)** Assess your model and recommend changes so that it will work in space. **(PSDR)** Justify why you built your station in space!
What colours have you chosen for the exterior and interior of the station? Show why you have chosen these colours. Now paint both the outside and inside of the station.	Compare one of the planets and space (Venn Diagram). Will this help explain why you have chosen to build your station in space?		Review the colours that you have chosen and justify why you have chosen them.
Make a model of the solar system to scale. On your scale, use one Astronomical Unit (1 Au) = 149.6 million km. Earth = 1 Au Prepare various tasty menus that will help your workers in reducing loss of calcium. Will the **W Chart** be of any value to you?	Select the materials that you will need to build your space station. On what basis will you be choosing these materials? Arrange various physical exercises that your workers can do to prevent muscle 'wastage'.		One member of your team has very high blood pressure. Use **SCRAM** to modify the meals for them. Identify the best exercise for one of the workers who has very poor blood circulation. What will you recommend to workers who suffer from homesickness?

Continued on page 82

Example 2 (Cont.)

Eight ways to be smart	Bloom's taxonomy: Six thinking levels	
	Knowing	Understanding
Musical–rhythmic I enjoy making and listening to music	Listen to songs that relate to space. View films and videos that relate to space research.	Describe to your group the meaning of one of these songs.
Interpersonal–social I enjoy working with others	What traits do you have that will enable you to cope working in a close environment for months? Find out the maximum period of time that your workers can work in the space station. Is weightlessness a real issue? How will your workers deal with it?	How will you select the 50 workers? Write a job description for the space manager. Receive the applications, short list and then interview the applicants.
Intrapersonal–intuitive I enjoy working by myself	How do you feel when you watch TV and you see astronauts working inside the International Space Station?	Tomorrow you will be interviewed for the position of space station manager. Use **X** or **Y chart** to prepare yourself for this interview.
Naturalist I enjoy caring for plants and animals	Which plants are likely to survive and thrive in the space station?	On board the space station there is a small cat/dog. Explain how you are going to keep this animal healthy.

Continued on page 83

Transferring the knowledge to the real world

Bloom's taxonomy: Six thinking levels			
Applying	Analysing	Creating	Evaluating
Examine songs, CDs and film clips that can be used to entertain the workers on the space station.	Arrange the music that will be available to your workers on the space station.	**Real Assessment Task** The year is 2020. Due to poor diet and insufficient, physical exercise, many children are becoming obese and developing diabetes. The WDC* wants to build a factory in space to produce large amounts of insulin. Your job is to prepare a model of a space station that will employ 50 people. In addition, you will advise the WDC on how you will look after these workers in terms of housing, food, clothing, exercises and music. (*WDC: World Diabetes Council)	Play this music to your class. Then, use the **LDC** strategy to evaluate how this music has been received by the other students.
Use your own concept or mind map to teach a younger student about the solar system or your space station. Was your concept/mind map successful? How do you know? You may choose to use the **LDC** strategy to receive some feedback from the other student.	Choose the **A&R**, **ARC** or **The Rake** to solve conflicts that are likely to develop when individuals work in close areas.		Interview the manager of your space station or the person that manages NASA. Review how well you have worked as a group and recommend improvements. **(TPSS)**
Complete your own concept or mind map to see how much you have learned about the solar system.	Investigate how space travel affects the human body. What can be done to prevent these problems?	Impersonate your favourite astronaut. **(X chart)**	Evaluate your life as the manager of the space station. Write an autobiography titled 'A day in the life of'.
Make a collection of all the available material relating to space exploration and share it with your class.	Use a **Venn diagram** to compare and contrast life on Earth and on the space station.	Estimate how many small plants are needed to produce enough oxygen to keep one person alive.	Determine how your space station can operate in a way that will make the least damage to the environment.

83

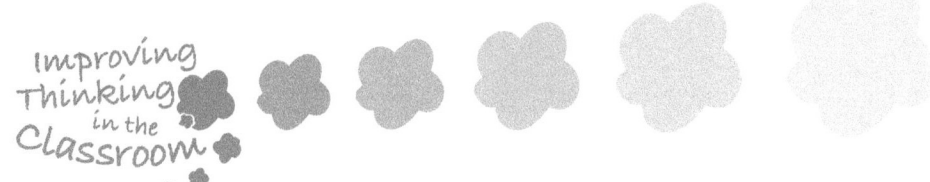

Example 3: Plants (Year level: ESL, K–1 & Children with Learning Difficulties)

Eight ways to be smart	Bloom's taxonomy: Six thinking levels		
	Pre-Knowing	Knowing	Understanding
Verbal–linguistic I enjoy reading, writing and speaking	**Kinds of Plants:** **Nouns** trees bush grass flowers shrubs **Verbs** be chop cover cut die dig eat grow have plant put water **Propositions** in/on under/above beside between	Name the parts of a plant.	Explain how plants grow.
Logical–mathematical I enjoy working with numbers and science		List all the known plants	How many species are there?
Visual–spatial I enjoy painting, drawing and visualising		Bring your favourite plant to class.	Draw your own plant.
Body–kinesthetic I enjoy doing hands-on activities, sports and dance		Participate in an excursion to the Botanical Gardens/local park.	Describe the kind of plants that you saw during the excursion.

Continued on page 85

Transferring the knowledge to the real world

| Bloom's taxonomy: Six thinking levels ||||
Applying	Analysing	Creating	Evaluating
Read a Big Book about Trees.	Analyse the Big Book about Trees. What did you like most about this book? Why?	**Real Assessment Task One** After reading the Enormous Turnip, create your own narrative.	Read your narrative in front of the class and receive their feedback using the LDC.
Examine the things that plants need in order to survive.	Discover how your plant grows.	Keep record of your plant growth.	Evaluate the growth of your plant every week.
Label the parts of your plant.	Compare the plants in your country with plants that are found in Australia.	Design a Venn Diagram using the information that you already have.	Are the plants found in your country different to the ones found in Australia?
Walk around the school grounds and look at the plants.	Compare and contrast the plants in your school grounds with those that you saw during the excursion.	**Real Assessment Task Two** Create a box where you will be able to grow your chosen small plant.	Evaluate the process of making your own box. How could you improve it?

Continued on page 86

Example 3 (Cont.)

Eight ways to be smart	Bloom's taxonomy: Six thinking levels		
	Pre-Knowing	Knowing	Understanding
Musical–rhythmic I enjoy making and listening to music		Listen to songs about plants/forests/environment.	Explain the meaning of your chosen song to your group.
Interpersonal–social I enjoy working with others		What did you like the most about the excursion to the Botanical Gardens?	Share your thoughts with your partner (TPS).
Intrapersonal–intuitive I enjoy working by myself		Read a simple worksheet about plants.	Complete simple worksheets about plants.
Naturalist I enjoy caring for plants and animals		List the parts of a plant: branch stem fruit petals flower leaf roots seeds trunk	Explain why plants need light: light soil sun water

Continued on page 87

Transferring the knowledge to the real world

Bloom's taxonomy: Six thinking levels			
Applying	Analysing	Creating	Evaluating
Sing this song in English.	Using various instruments, begin to compose your own song/dance.	Create your own song/dance.	Present this song/dance to your class (LDC).
In your group, discuss the things that plants need to grow.	What would have happened if your plant did not receive any light? (PSDR)	**Real Assessment Task Three** Devise an experiment that will show what happens when plants do not receive any light.	How could you have improved your experiment? Share your suggestion with your class.
Match the words with the pictures.	Using the Y or X Chart share with your team how you feel when a tree is cut down.	Create a dictionary of plants (in English & in your own language).	Using your dictionary, teach another child what you have learned about plants.
Examine why these animals are associated with plants: ant bee beetle butterfly ladybird spider grasshopper	Categorise the animals that are associated with plants.	Plant your favourite vegetable in the school garden.	Advise on how you could improve growing vegetables.

87

Case study

The integrated project detailed in this section was trialled with a group of year 6, 7 and 8 students. The children were drawn from a number of primary schools and secondary schools and met for two hours every Tuesday afternoon. The schools are located in an area characterised by high unemployment and a large number of single parent families receiving welfare support. There are some light to medium industries in the area. About 20 kilometres away there are two large seaside communities with marinas which receive a large number of local, interstate and international tourists each year, many arriving by boat.

The schools teach a 'traditional' curriculum. The eight key learning areas (KLAs) are taught independent of each other. Instruction is mainly teacher directed with students spending much of their time copying material from the blackboard and memorising a great deal of information to be assessed through regular pencil-paper tests.

The project was implemented primarily to address these children's poor academic performance, high level of disengagement and low level of motivation. Their behaviour could best be referred to as 'challenging'.

Having considered all the strategies that the schools could implement to re-engage these students, the decision was made to restructure the curriculum so that students would be working through an integrated project culminating in a real assessment task.

The integrated project aimed to:

- improve students academic performance, engagement and motivation
- reduce behaviour concerns
- provide useful and practical strategies on how boat builders could market their boats.

It was also decided to implement this project in two phases. During Phase 1 the students would design, build and assess their boat. During Phase 2 the students would market their boat through a real assessment task.

Phase 1: Design, build and assess your boat.

An integral part of this project was preparing a short report summarising what they had learned. Opposite is a copy of the final report that was handed in by a group of students.

Phase 2: marketing your boat

This phase of the case study, the integrated project titled 'Marketing your boat' (pp. 90–91), encouraged the students to show significant intellectual accomplishments by creating a report/video/website/computer program in order to market their boat. In order for the students to complete their assessment task, they constructed knowledge, carried out disciplined inquiry and connected their learning to the world outside the classroom.

Transferring the knowledge to the real world

Report: My life as a boat

My story starts as a balsa tree growing in the jungles of Brazil. Upon reaching maturity, I was cut down and then shipped to Australia.

After I was unloaded at the Sydney docks, I was sent to a factory where I was prefabricated into sections that could be assembled into a small boat.

I was then transported to a store in Brisbane and there I sat for a long time on a dusty shelf until a group of students purchased me.

The students, having read the instructions, were able to identify the keel and the transoms and thus commenced assembling me into a boat.

Unfortunately, the keel had been glued on the wrong way therefore it had to be reconstructed (you can imagine how painful this was to me!). The sides were glued to transoms 1, 2 and 3, and the hull was stuck to the bottom of the transoms. This took much longer than had been expected because the hull and the sides had to be bent into proper position (ouch! It hurts.) Then, the prow was glued on top of the sides.

Once the boat had been built, the students decided that I needed to be painted. I was first given a white undercoat and my surface had to be lightly sanded between each successive coat in order to remove any rough spots. (On a dry day, sand paper can be very painful indeed!) I am very pleased with my final colours.

- Prow – orange
- Bow – white
- Seats – blue

To make me look attractive, a number of decorative stickers were placed on me.

The students were keen for me to move around, thus they purchased a motor kit which contained an outboard motor and a battery box. Would you believe that two C-type batteries were needed to move me? The students learned that by connecting 'like' coloured wires, I moved forward and that by reversing the wires I moved backwards.

To my horror, during my first trial, I sank straight to the bottom of the tank.

At my expense, they learned that there was not enough water in the small tank to hold me. Luckily for me one of the students had a swimming pool and to my delight, all future tests were carried out in it. Oh I feel so much better now!

Case study: Marketing your boat (Year level: 6–10)

Eight ways to be smart	Bloom's taxonomy: Six thinking levels		
	Knowing	Understanding	Applying
Verbal–linguistic I enjoy reading, writing and speaking	8. Brainstorm all the different types of boats. 24. What are the different ways that you can sell a product? **(mindmap)**.	25. Explain different ways that you can employ to sell a product. 26. Describe one of your favourite ads. Why is it effective?	49. Prepare the necessary ads, brochures, videos, webpages, public presentations, media releases & feature stories **(BROW)**.
Logical–mathematical I enjoy working with numbers and science	10. Review issues dealing with measurements & place value. 3. State what we mean by floating & sinking.	1. Use the **PSDR** method to predict what will happen to the various fruits & vegetables when placed in water (see activity 23). 4. How will you float a potato in the centre of the bucket without using any strings or weights? **(WINCE)**.	20. How much will you have to sell your boat in order to make a profit? **(Trec/RedMast)**. 2. Carry out activity 23. (Why do some objects float & others sink?). Use the **PSDR** Method.
Visual–spatial I enjoy painting, drawing and visualising	20. Look at various boats. 21. Locate various menus that can be used on your boat.	22. Draw your own model boat. 23. Outline the various menus that will be available on your boat.	16. Choose the designs & paints for your boat. 31. Illustrate your menus **(W Chart)**.
Body–kinesthetic I enjoy doing hands-on activities, sports and dance	29. Find out what types of hobbies and sports passengers can play on board a boat.	30. Describe the main hobbies and sports that can be played on board a boat.	35. Show how one of these hobbies & sports are played. 14. Complete Activity 51 (Build or reassemble your boat).
Musical–rhythmic I enjoy making and listening to music	36. Name the type of music and entertainment that is usually available to passengers on board boats.	37. Match the type of music and entertainment to people of different ages.	39. Choose the music & entertainment that will be available to passengers on your boat.
Interpersonal–social I enjoy working with others	11. Review basic rules of working with others.	12. How are the different roles going to be assigned? Who will decide?	23. Working as a group, now commence your Marketing Plan.
Intrapersonal–intuitive I enjoy working by myself	21. How do you feel when you are on board a boat? **(LDC)**.	49. Express your feeling whilst on a boat in very rough seas. **(Y chart)**	15. Share with another student your excitement when your boat actually floated.
Naturalist I enjoy caring for plants and animals	54. List all the items that you will need to take on board such as binoculars, running shoes, mosquito repellent, sunscreen lotion, hat and suitable clothing.	33. Draw and/or photograph plants, animals and scenic sites whilst the boat is moving from one location to another and during the time that you are allowed on land.	15. Organise your own portfolio where you will keep your written observations, drawings, collections & photographs.

Continued on page 91

Transferring the knowledge to the real world

Bloom's taxonomy: Six Thinking Levels		
Analysing	Creating	Evaluating
6. Analyse the best way to market your boat. 7. Compare and contrast the best and the worst ad that you have seen.	**Real assessment task:** Create a report/video/ website/computer program titled 'Marketing your boat'.	8. Assess your report/video/website/ computer program. **(LDC)** 9. Present your Project to your class and receive feedback (use a criteria sheet).
16. Identify the major issues that you had to deal with in floating the potato in the centre of the bucket? **(TAP)**	17. Estimate the cost of building your boat by including materials, labour and advertising. **(TREC/Red/Mast)**	18. Evaluate the **PSDR** method and **WINCE** strategy. Were these thinking tools of any value to you in solving these problems? 19. Justify why your boat floated in the pool but not in the small tank.
26. Use the **Venn diagram** to compare two very different boats/menus.	27. Investigate the best way to paint the boat in order to prevent it from rusting. **(TAP)**	28. Assess your final shape and colours of your boat. Discuss ways to improve the shape and the colours.
33. Categorise these hobbies and sports in terms of their value to senior passengers.	34. Identify the issues dealing with environmental health, safety, food requirements, fitness and sports.	35. Were your passengers satisfied with the food, hobbies and sports that were available to them? How do you know?
39. Survey the type of music and entertainment that teenagers enjoy whilst on holidays. Will this music be suitable to older passengers?	40. Working with your group, compose a song/rap/dance. **(LDC)**	41. Present your song/rap/dance. Is it appropriate for teenagers? Recommend any improvements.
45. How well did you work as a group? Survey every member of your group. **(TPSS)**	46. Devise a questionnaire to find out if your passengers are satisfied with the food/customer service/hobbies.	47. Evaluate the impact that your boat is likely to have on the environment. **(The Rake)**
51. Investigate your life as a boat builder!	52. Impersonate your favourite Captain. **(X chart)**	53. Carry out a **SOWC analysis** on the possible success of your boat business.
57. Select books, videos, CDs, films and nature simulations programs that will be available on board. On what basis will you select this material?	58. Create a map indicating nature walks, bird sites, rock formations, mountains, beach areas & tourist attractions that are located near the various places visited by the boat.	59. How difficult are these 'areas of interest' for people of different ages and mobility? Eg. are they accessible to people in wheelchairs? Rate them and then recommend changes.

In conclusion

Teaching is such a wonderful profession because it enables you to share your own unique set of experiences with your children. The 48 and 56-grid matrix allows teachers to choose how they are going to organise the material in order to engage each and every student! As required, they will demonstrate the mandated learning outcomes. However, different teachers will be able to choose how they are going to 'weave their own magic' by choosing the order in which the activities will be completed.

In addition, teachers can use the 48 and 56-grid matrix to reflect on their practices by:

- aligning real assessment tasks, learning outcomes, activities, thinking tools and quality teaching principles

- determining if their units are 'balanced'; that is, if their activities are spread out throughout Bloom's taxonomy's six levels of thinking or are they clustered in the low levels or in the higher order thinking skills area?

- reflecting on the children's level of on-task behaviour. In other words, how much time did the teacher have to spend on discipline problems? Were the children engaged through their preferred learning styles?

- scanning the grid for 'evidence' that the elements of quality teaching/essential of learnings have been demonstrated.

- evaluating the students' real assessment tasks to verify whether these show 'depth' and 'rigour'

- recommending additions/deletions to be made to the unit in the event that it will be taught again.

Undeniably, the 48 and 56-grid matrix provides you with an enormous capacity to nurture your students' thinking needs whilst simultaneously engaging your children through their preferred learning styles.

In conclusion

Teachers' reflections on the 48 and 56-grid matrix

Given the fact that since 1997 this matrix has been implemented in hundreds of schools throughout Australia and New Zealand, we are now able to summarise the benefits of using this grid. The following comments have been made by teachers who have participated in workshops titled 'Improving your children's learning outcomes' and then proceeded to use it as their curriculum framework. So, what do these classroom teachers have to say?

1. Especially useful for students in mixed ability classes because it allows the children to work at different levels.

2. Concise, comprehensive, simplified and streamlined.

3. Extremely useful because it enables me to see if I cater for the range of learning styles in class as well as making learning stimulating.

4. A terrific framework. I can see each child with their own individualised spreadsheet for a unit!

5. Will be valuable as a source of reference to 'lift the learning to a higher plane'. It will encourage me to 'step up' for those children who require it.

6. The matrix will enable me to devise a bigger range of activities which allow the students more selection and ownership of their learning.

Additional comments can be viewed at <www.pli.com.au> under 'Teachers Reflections'.

What about educators? What do they say about the matrix?

Here is what Bruce McCourt, Senior Education Officer, has to say 'You inspired the Design and Technology teacher who was at her wits end about how to engage her Year 7 students. Her 'well I've nothing to lose' approach prompted her to design a unit on computing skills that literally changed the culture, commitment and engagement of her students. Attendance, completion of work, behaviour and demonstrable learning outcomes increased dramatically as a result of your work.'

Jodie Clark (Primary School Teacher - New South Wales) says:

"The effect of using the matrix on our teaching has been astounding. The major differences we have seen come in the form of student engagement and improved learning outcomes for all learners." (The Matrix, The West Australian Education Magazine Term 4, 2005).

Andrew Grant (Primary School Teacher - Queensland) says:

"I have been planning with the matrix for three years now and I have found them to be an excellent system for inclusive planning. The students love the matrix, as they are full of varied activities that they have a choice in. The more I use the matrix in my classroom, the more I discover about them and the wonderful impact they can have on planning and the interest level of the children." (The Matrix, The West Australian Education Magazine Term 4, 2005).

Tony Merritt (Deputy Principal - Australian Capital Territory) says:

"So what's the secret about the matrix? Merritt says that teachers at his school find of most benefit is the easy-to-use format of the matrix, that is designed so that students of all ages and abilities remain actively engaged in their learning. The matrices provide students of all ability levels the opportunity to participate, as they are able to choose activities that are of particular interest to them, as well as completing the core activities." (Curriculum Development, Teacher, July 2005).

Paul Carreiro (Principal - New South Wales) says:

"The matrix has become an outstanding learning tool for our teachers, Carreiro says. A well-planned matrix has the ability to cater for all levels of children in the class with varied abilities since the matrix takes children along on their journey of learning. The implementation in our school has been excellent." (Curriculum Development, Teacher, July 2005).

Allan Greenbank (High School Teacher - South Australia) says:

"I use the Bloom and Gardner overview as advocated by Ralph to provide richness, depth, intellectual rigour, flexibility and relevance to students' learning. The techniques that Ralph teaches and advocates have a profound impact on classroom and outcomes for students. This is because he packages good pedagogy with tried and proven teaching methods. What he does is not theoretical, ivory tower idealism but rather a practical method that makes teaching and planning easier so that teachers can get on with the job of guiding students along their development continua." (The Matrix, The West Australian Education Magazine Term 4, 2005).

Jenny Bellenger (Primary School Teacher - New South Wales) says:

"Over the last two years we have been investigating and researching ways we can best meet the needs of students in the 21st century. After attending Ralph's workshop, I was energised because for the first time I could see how valuable the matrix is as it incorporates all the important components such as catering for individual differences and abilities, embedding technology, utilising thinking tools, including the quality teaching aspects and using rubrics and rich assessment tasks to drive learning. All these are included in the matrix through cleverly layering them into the grid. I would call that value adding." (The Matrix, The West Australian Education Magazine Term 4, 2005).

In conclusion

For Samantha Underdown, a dance teacher at a large Gold Coast High School and Arts Coordinator for the Gold Coast District, the matrix has made an enormous contribution to the intellectual rigour of her teaching. Underdown points out that the matrix is easy to understand and therefore easily shared amongst teachers at the same or different schools. (Curriculum Development, Teacher, July 2005).

For Brigid Daly, a middle school teacher in the Northern Territory, the grid has really simplified student-centred learning, making it accessible to busy teachers. It also allows students to build up to higher-order thinking, gradually working their way through a learning unit to the higher-order thinking assessment items. Daly has also found that the grid encourages students to reflect on their own learning, making "meta-cognition" more than just a word to be heard at conferences or seen in policy documents. Students use the grid to learn more about themselves, their preferred learning styles and how to engage in different levels of thinking. Daly says this improves their self esteem, as they discover that they are intelligent, and can critically analyse, create and evaluate: what a great gift to give them! (Curriculum Development, Teacher, July 2005).

A number of additional letters can be viewed at <www.pli.com.au> under 'Testimonials'.

APPENDIX

Check your thinking answers
Bloom's taxonomy: Activity 1

Students learning experiences	K	U	Ap	An	C	E
1. List all the people in the story.	*					
2. Evaluate the research on AIDS.						*
3. Name the capital of Indonesia.	*					
4. Locate all the parks in your suburb.	*					
5. Look at the clock and tell me the time.	*					
6. Retell this from the point view of the villain.		*				
7. Draw pictures to show how plants and animals interact together.		*				
8. Illustrate the main ideas of the book.			*			
9. Complete a flow chart showing the various stages of bread making.			*			
10. Design a cover for a magazine.					*	
11. Convert this word problem into a mathematical statement.		*				
12. Outline your plans for your next project.		*				
13. Construct an ecological foodchain and foodweb.					*	
14. Classify the following organisms into their correct Phyla.				*		
15. Make a clay model of a volcano.				*		
16. Survey your friends in terms of their eating habits.				*		
17. Solve the following maths problem and show all your calculations.			*			
18. Make a scrapbook about …				*		
19. Translate this sentence from English into French.		*				

Appendix

Students learning experiences	K	U	Ap	An	C	E
20. Write your home address.	*					
21. Recommend new strategies to be adopted based on your SOWC analysis.						*
22. Categorise these items into plastic and metal.					*	
23. Make a family tree showing all the important relationships.			*			
24. Compare and contrast Asian and African elephants.				*		
25. Determine whether this novel is suitable for secondary school students.						*
26. Review a work of art in terms of form, colour and texture.						*
27. Construct a graph to illustrate the following relationship.					*	
28. Devise a number of ways to improve …					*	
29. Calculate how many metres of wire is needed to fence a paddock with the following dimensions …			*			
30. Invent a machine that will be able to do a certain task.					*	
31. Compose a rhythm or add new words to a well-known tune.					*	
32. Devise an experiment that will extract more iron from its ore.					*	
33. Write the formula for photosynthesis.	*					
34. Retell the story in your own words.		*				
35. Design a solar energy car.					*	
36. Conduct a survey to gather information about teenage smoking.					*	
37. Organise and conduct a debate dealing with a controversial issue.						*
38. Discuss factors that should be considered when buying toys for your children.						*
39. Justify why you have chosen this particular piece of music for your school play						*
40. List all the information that you remember about the Second World War.	*					
41. Make a flowchart to show the critical stages of …				*		
42. Construct a model of the DNA molecule.					*	

Multiple Intelligences Test: MIT

Introduction

Why write another Multiple Intelligences Test (MIT)?

Basically, all the existing MI tests are based on the assumption that teachers will administer these tests to their students without ever taking into consideration the teachers' own Multiple Intelligences.

Whilst this enables teachers to discover their students' Multiple Intelligences, often this knowledge has not led to any real change in the way teachers engage with their students in the classroom.

Undeniably, this test takes a complete different and novel approach to Multiple Intelligences testing.

In fact, the underlying philosophy of this test is that teachers and students are 'partners' in learning thus both their Multiple Intelligences must be taken into consideration. It follows that teachers should be prepared to complete this test first in order to discover their own Cluster of Multiple Intelligences (CMI) and their own RAMP (Ralph's Area of Maximum Potential). Then, having discovered their CMI, they should proceed to administer this test to their students to find out the children's 'preferred multiple intelligences'. Finally, by aligning their Cluster of Multiple Intelligences and their RAMP with those of their children, they will be in an outstanding position to fully engage all their students. Imagine the impact that this alignment is going to have in the way teachers provide for their students' preferred learning styles? Wow!

In order to discover your Cluster of preferred multiple intelligences and your RAMP, we are going to rely on Gardner's Theory of Multiple Intelligences which argues that:

- all humans can be smart in at least eight different ways
- each intelligence is located in certain areas of our brains, and
- we use a combination of multiple intelligences in order to deal with issues in our lives and to solve problems.

Appendix

One way to discover your "preferred multiple intelligences" is to complete the following test. Read each statement and then place a tick or a cross on a scale 1 to 5 (1 means that you do not enjoy this activity very much and 5 means that you enjoy this activity a great deal).

Statements	Scale				
	1	2	3	4	5
Section 1: Verbal/linguistic intelligence					
I enjoy reading and writing stories					
I enjoy reading and writing poetry, poems & plays					
I enjoy entertaining others by telling stories and jokes					
I enjoy keeping a diary					
I enjoy making speeches and arguing my point of view					
I enjoy attending plays and drama productions					
I enjoy participating in discussions, public speaking and debates					
I enjoy creating a newspaper, radio, internet or TV advertisement					
I enjoy writing and editing a class magazine					
I enjoy learning a new language					
Total Points					

Statements	Scale				
	1	2	3	4	5
Section 2: Logical/mathematical intelligence					
I enjoy solving mathematical problems					
I enjoy carrying out many different types of mathematical calculations					
I enjoy using computers to make calculations and spreadsheets					
I enjoy creating computer programs					
I enjoy analysing and interpreting data					
I enjoy classifying plants and animals					
I enjoy thinking logically in order to figure out why things work the way they do in the natural world					
I enjoy performing science experiments					
I enjoy collecting plant and animal specimens and classify them					
I enjoy setting up & maintaining fish tanks, aquariums and terrariums					
Total Points					

Statements	Scale				
	1	2	3	4	5
Section 3: Visual/spatial intelligence					
I enjoy painting, drawing and sketching					
I enjoy having access to art books, photos, puzzles, videos & films					
I enjoy creating accurate maps and graphic designs					
I enjoy remembering where words & pictures are placed on a page					
I enjoy illustrating books, reports, magazines and newsletters					
I enjoy designing diagrams and graphs					
I enjoy preparing flyers, posters, collages, maps, mazes & murals					
I enjoy designing the graphics for newspaper/magazine/radio/internet and TV advertisements					
I enjoy showing my emotions by using facial expressions					
I enjoy visiting art galleries					
Total Points					

Statements	Scale				
	1	2	3	4	5
Section 4: Bodily/kinaesthetic intelligence					
I enjoy dancing and teach others how to dance					
I enjoy learning dances from various cultural groups					
I enjoy creating my own dances and performing them in front of my class					
I enjoy playing sports and doing physical exercises					
I enjoy participating in swimming, athletic and sports carnivals					
I enjoy building and repairing models, games, crafts & props					
I enjoy maintaining gardens and rainforest areas					
I enjoy acting out scenes					
I enjoy imitating others					
I enjoy attending sporting events, dance competitions and crafts shows					
Total Points					

Appendix

Statements	Scale				
	1	2	3	4	5
Section 5: Musical/rhythmic intelligence					
I enjoy listening to many kinds of music					
I enjoy remembering tunes and melodies					
I enjoy playing a musical instrument					
I enjoy having a variety of musical instruments, tapes, CDs, soundtracks and tapes					
I enjoy singing and creating new songs, jingles, operas, performances and compositions					
I enjoy participating in choirs, music clubs and music bands					
I enjoy creating my own melodies, sound effects and raps					
I enjoy composing my own music on computers					
I enjoy singing and/or playing a musical instrument in front of my class					
I enjoy attending various concerts					
Total Points					

Statements	Scale				
	1	2	3	4	5
Section 6: Interpersonal/social intelligence					
I enjoy working with others					
I enjoy caring for other children					
I enjoy organising other people					
I enjoy resolving conflicts and building friendships					
I enjoy being involved in drama and role plays					
I enjoy helping younger children to complete their school work					
I enjoy volunteering to work with communities groups					
I enjoy joining committees and social clubs					
I enjoy debating controversial issues					
I enjoy celebrating important events like birthdays					
Total Points					

Statements	Scale				
	1	2	3	4	5
Section 7: Intrapersonal/intuitive intelligence					
I enjoy working alone					
I enjoy completing projects by myself					
I enjoy having the opportunity to choose the activities that I would like to do					
I enjoy keeping a journal					
I enjoy reading diaries and autobiographies					
I enjoy choosing various areas in the classroom to work in					
I enjoy meditating, setting up goals and reflecting					
I enjoy knowing my feelings, emotions, strengths and weaknesses					
I enjoy expressing my emotions and my opinions					
I enjoy setting up my own goals					
Total Points					

Statements	Scale				
	1	2	3	4	5
Section 8: Naturalist intelligence					
I enjoy caring for plants and animals					
I enjoy keeping a pet in the classroom					
I enjoy establishing a small garden and a recycling program					
I enjoy going on field trips, nature walks and visits to museums					
I enjoy collecting and classifying natural specimens into collections					
I enjoy establishing a weather station and graph the temperature for a week/month					
I enjoy debating issues relating to conservation issues and joining an environmental club					
I enjoy reading stories and watching shows that deal with animals and natural events					
I enjoy organising my individual nature portfolio where I can store my animals and plants' specimens, field notes, photos and drawings					
I enjoy listening to guest speakers from groups such as Greening Australia, local recycling firms, zoo keepers, organic farmers and environmentalists					
Total Points					

Appendix

In completing this test, most likely you have found that you have different scores for each of the multiple intelligences. Now, transfer your points to the Multiple Intelligences Chart from highest to lowest.

Multiple Intelligence Chart

Order	Score	Intelligence
1 (highest)		
2		
3		
4		
5		
6		
7		
8 (lowest)		

At this stage, select the three intelligences where you have the three highest scores and place their names on the following overlapping circles:

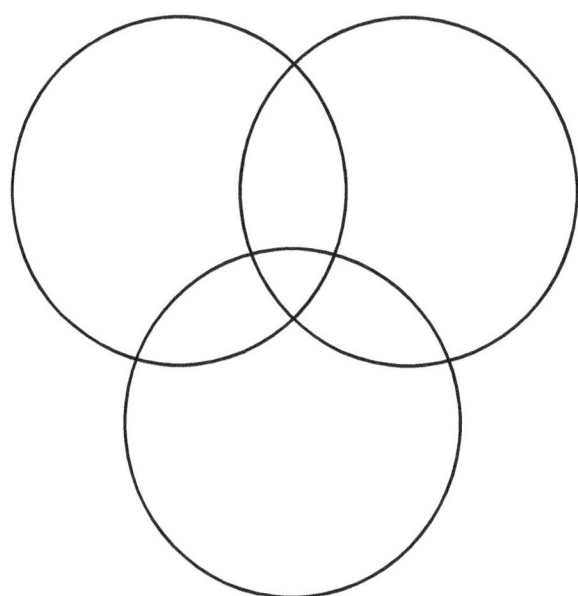

This represents your present "Cluster" of intelligences. It means that in solving problems and in dealing with the world around you, you use a combination of these three intelligences rather than just one. However, this does not mean that the other five intelligences do not exist in your brain. What it means is that presently these three intelligences are the most developed.

You are now ready to colour in the centre of these overlapping circles using your favourite colour. In doing so, you will discover your RAMP, that is, your Area of Maximum Potential.

The concept of RAMP (Ralph's Area of Maximum Potential) was first introduced by Ralph Pirozzo in 2005).

Based on your RAMP, you are likely to do your best work whilst using these three multiple intelligences. For example, if your three most developed intelligences were Verbal/linguistic, Visual/spatial & Interpersonal then you are most likely to do your best work when sharing what you know about a certain topic with your classmates using language, charts, drawings, maps and posters.

Of what value is knowing your Cluster of Intelligences and your RAMP to you/your parents/friends/teachers/future partners & employers?

_____
_____
_____
_____
_____
_____
_____
_____
_____
_____
_____

Please note that your Cluster of Intelligences and your RAMP are not in "cement". In other words, they are likely to change depending on a number of factors including:

- age
- different experiences
- friends
- hobbies
- jobs
- partners
- people that you will meet
- travel

References

Armstrong, T. (1994). *Multiple Intelligences in the Classroom*. Alexandria, Virginia: Asssociation for Supervision and Curriculum Development.

Armstrong, T. (2000). *Multiple Intelligences in the Classroom Second Edition*. Alexandria, Virginia: Asssociation for Supervision and Curriculum Development.

Darling-Hammond, L. (2001). *Educational Research and Educational Reform: Drawing the Connections between Research, Policy and Practice*. Invited Address, AERA Conference, Seattle, 10–14 April.

Fogarty, R. & Stoehr, J. (1995). *Integrating curricula with multiple intelligences: Teams, themes and threads*. Melbourne, Australia: Hawker Brownlow Education.

Gardner, H. & Hatch, T. (1989). Multiple intelligences go to school: Educational implications of the theory of multiple intelligences. *Educational Researcher*, 18 (8), 4–10.

Gardner, H. (1983). *Frames of Mind*. London: Fontana Press.

Gardner, H. (1999). *Intelligences Reframed: Multiple Intelligences for the 21st Century*. New York, New York: Basic Books.

Gibbs, J. (2001). *Tribes: A new way of learning and being together*. Windsor, California: CenterSource Systems.

Lovat, T. (2003). What is Quality Teaching? *Directions in Education, Australian Council for Educational Leaders*, 12(20), 1.

McCourt, B. (2002). Private correspondence.

New South Wales Department of Education and Training (2003). *Quality Teaching in NSW Public Schools: Discussion Paper*. New South Wales, Sydney: Department of Education and Training.

Newmann, F.M. & Associates. (1996). *Authentic Achievement: Restructuring Schools for Intellectual Quality*. San Francisco: Jossey-Bass.

Queensland Department of Education (2001). *The Queensland School Reform Longitudinal Study Final Report (QSRLS)*. Brisbane: Education Queensland.

Queensland Department of Education (2002). *A Guide to Productive Pedagogies: Classroom Reflection Manual*. Brisbane: Education Queensland.

Silver, H., Strong, R. & Perini, M. (2000). *So Each May Learn - Integrating Learning Styles and Multiple Intelligences*. Alexandria, Virginia: Association for Supervision and Curriculum Development.

Vialle, W. & Perry, J. (1995). *Nurturing Multiple Intelligences in the Australian Classroom*. Melbourne, Australia: Hawker Brownlow Education.

www.ingramcontent.com/pod-product-compliance
Lightning Source LLC
Chambersburg PA
CBHW081918090526
44590CB00019B/3397